What People Are Saying
about the Left Behind Series

"This is the most successful Christian-fiction series ever."
—Publishers Weekly

"Tim LaHaye and Jerry B. Jenkins . . . are doing for Christian fiction what John Grisham did for courtroom thrillers."
—TIME

"The authors' style continues to be thoroughly captivating and keeps the reader glued to the book, wondering what will happen next. And it leaves the reader hungry for more."
—Christian Retailing

"Combines Tom Clancy–like suspense with touches of romance, high-tech flash and Biblical references."
—The New York Times

"It's not your mama's Christian fiction anymore."
—The Dallas Morning News

"Wildly popular—and highly controversial."
—USA Today

"Bible teacher LaHaye and master storyteller Jenkins have created a believable story of what could happen after the Rapture. They present the gospel clearly without being preachy, the characters have depth, and the plot keeps the reader turning pages."
—Moody Magazine

"Christian thriller. Prophecy-based fiction. Juiced-up morality tale. Call it what you like, the Left Behind series . . . now has a label its creators could never have predicted: blockbuster success."
—Entertainment Weekly

Tyndale House products by Tim LaHaye and Jerry B. Jenkins

The Left Behind® book series
Left Behind®
Tribulation Force
Nicolae
Soul Harvest
Apollyon
Assassins
The Indwelling
The Mark
Desecration
The Remnant
Armageddon
Book 12—available spring 2004

Other Left Behind® products
Left Behind®: The Kids
Devotionals
Calendars
Abridged audio products
Dramatic audio products
Graphic novels
Gift books
and more . . .

Other Tyndale House books by Tim LaHaye and Jerry B. Jenkins
Perhaps Today
Are We Living in the End Times?

For the latest information on individual products, release
dates, and future projects, visit www.leftbehind.com

Tyndale House books by Tim LaHaye
How to Be Happy Though Married
Spirit-Controlled Temperament
Transformed Temperaments
Why You Act the Way You Do

Tyndale House books by Jerry B. Jenkins
And Then Came You
As You Leave Home
Still the One

THESE WILL NOT BE

INCREDIBLE STORIES OF LIVES TRANSFORMED
AFTER READING THE LEFT BEHIND NOVELS

LEFT BEHIND®

TIM LAHAYE
JERRY B. JENKINS

with *Norman B. Rohrer*

Tyndale House Publishers, Inc. Wheaton, Illinois

Visit Tyndale's exciting Web site at www.tyndale.com

Discover the latest about the Left Behind series at www.leftbehind.com

Designed by Julie Chen

Published in association with the literary agency of Alive Communications, Inc., 7680 Goddard Street, Suite 200, Colorado Springs, CO 80920.

Library of Congress Cataloging-in-Publication Data

LaHaye, Tim F.
     These will not be left behind : incredible stories of lives transformed after reading the Left behind novels / Tim Lahaye and Jerry B. Jenkins ; with Norman B. Rohrer.
         p. cm.
     ISBN 0-8423-6593-1 (sc)
     1. LaHaye, Tim F. Left behind series.   2. Christian fiction, American—Appreciation.
3. Rapture (Christian eschatology) 4. End of the world in literature.   5. Eschatology in literature.   6. Life change events.   7. Books and reading.   I. Jenkins, Jerry B.   II. Rohrer, Normal B.   III. Title.
     PS3562.A315 T48 2003
     813'.54—dc21   2003004054

Printed in the United States of America

07   06   05   04   03
5   4   3   2   1

To the new believers

Acknowledgments

To all who responded by faith to the Savior after reading the Left Behind novels, the Lord says, "You didn't choose me. I chose you" (John 15:16).

The friendships that developed during the writing of this book were not the result of our cleverness in finding one another, but rather of God's clear guidance. As C. S. Lewis writes in The Four Loves, *these friendships are "the instrument by which God reveals to each the beauty of all the others."*

It is my prayer that every reader will respond to the omnipotent power of our loving, forgiving God, who gave his Son as a sacrifice for our sins so that we all may be reconciled to him and not be left behind.

NORMAN B. ROHRER

CONTENTS

Introduction

Part One: Like a Mighty Army

Part Two: Just in Time

Part Three: Setting Prisoners Free

Part Four: Giving God the Glory

INTRODUCTION

Not since William E. Blackstone wrote *Jesus Is Coming* in 1878 has the church embraced Christian fiction with such passion as it has the Left Behind novels. The series shows the reader what our world could be like in the end times, when the prophecies of the Bible are fulfilled—beginning with the Rapture and ending with Armageddon and the return of Jesus Christ.

Hal Lindsey's nonfiction 1969 blockbuster, *The Late Great Planet Earth*, mapped out God's prophetic timetable and described how events seem to show that the end times are not far off. The suspenseful movie *A Thief in the Night*, created and produced by Russell S. Doughten Jr. and Donald W. Thompson in 1972, graphically portrayed the rapture of the church. But no book or movie has ever evoked such an immense reader response as the Left Behind novels.

Who are these millions and millions of readers? Why is there such interest in each new novel in the series when it is released? Some readers have said that they are reading each book as many as three times between releases. Many have responded to the message of these books: Don't be left behind after the Rapture! Readers who were already believers have come to a fuller and more meaningful understanding of the New Testament book of Revelation.

A pastor in Illinois, while reading the signature first volume in the series, suddenly felt compelled to visit his cancer-stricken neighbor. After reading to him from the novel, he urged his friend to open his heart and receive Christ as Savior. The neighbor eagerly said the sinner's prayer and reached out in faith to trust the Lord. A few hours later, he died.

An atheist in Great Britain surrendered his doubts and opened his hard heart to Christ while reading *Tribulation Force*, the second volume in the series.

A group of women in a Georgia rest home proclaimed tearfully, "We don't want to be *left behind!*" after listening to a visitor read from the first book of the series.

An alcoholic in Boston read the message in these books and trusted Christ because, as he said, "I want to see my mother in heaven."

Former drug addicts are overcoming the habits that have enslaved them and are finding hope and joy. The difficulties faced and defeated by Rayford, Chloe, and Buck in the Left Behind series have given them the vision and courage to confront their own troubles.

Young readers are becoming aware of the exciting opportunities and responsibilities of being a Christian after reading the novels in the kids' series. There will be forty titles when Left Behind: The Kids is complete. Encouraging reports are coming in from youngsters everywhere as they read and share these stories with other young people who need to hear about the free gift of salvation God offers them in Jesus Christ.

In addition, thousands of readers felt compelled to share about their changed lives on the www.leftbehind.com Web site. Many of their thoughts are contained in the E-notes feature included after each story in this book.

Is there someone you know who should read these stories so they won't be left behind? Could it be you?

The characters in the Left Behind series are fictional, but the people whose stories are featured in this book are real. *These Will Not Be Left Behind* describes how many have found the redeeming grace of Jesus Christ as a result of this powerful series. These dramatic stories about their decisions to make life-changing commitments give glory and honor to God.

As you read, pray for yourself, for your family, and for every person you meet, that all will surrender to Jesus Christ, our Savior and Lord.

> It was not long after [Jesus] said this that he was taken up into the sky while they were watching, and he disappeared into a cloud. As they were

straining their eyes to see him, two white-robed men suddenly stood there among them. They said, "Men of Galilee, why are you standing here staring at the sky? Jesus has been taken away from you into heaven. And someday, just as you saw him go, he will return!" (Acts 1:9-11)

PART ONE

LIKE A MIGHTY ARMY

I stand at the door and knock.

If you hear me calling and open the door,

I will come in, and we will share a meal as friends.

Revelation 3:20

EVEN IF IT
KILLS ME

EVEN BEFORE YOU BEGIN

YOUR ATTACK,

WHILE YOUR PLANS ARE

RIPENING LIKE GRAPES . . .

—ISAIAH 18:5

Darlene Snyder kissed her mother good-bye in Littleton, Colorado, climbed into her van, and started the engine. Ahead lay three hours of travel on Interstate 70 over the Front Range, past beautiful scenery like Mount Elbert's 14,431-foot peak (the state's highest), and then on to Glenwood Springs in time to prepare for work the next day cleaning

homes of the wealthy and famous in Aspen and
Snowmass.

Her mother, widowed when Darlene was still a
toddler, watched her daughter fondly from the door-
way of her home, remembering better days—the
days before Darlene ran away at sixteen; before her
husband died of colon cancer at the age of thirty-
three, at the peak of his ministry as a pastor; before
the years of drug addiction and all that went with it,
which Satan used to rob Darlene of her godly heritage.

In the glove box of the van was a set of four cassettes
entitled *Left Behind*—the audio version of a book by the
same title about events described in the last book of the
Bible. "Darlene!" her mother called, "have you listened
to the tapes yet?"

"Someday," Darlene said. She threw her mother
a kiss and sped away.

Weeks later, when she was returning home from a
doctor's appointment in Denver, Darlene popped the
first cassette into her player and turned up the volume.
As she listened, the Bible messages she'd heard as a
youngster returned to her mind. She most certainly
would be left behind when the Lord called her mother,
her brother and sisters, and their families home to
heaven. She thought of her father's love for the Savior
and how he had preached about him from the pulpit
of Union Gospel Church in Waterloo, Iowa, where she
was born. Before long, Darlene could hardly see the
road through her tears. As she struggled with unhappy

memories, she considered where her years of rebellion
had taken her. Somewhere in the Rocky Mountains of
Colorado, conviction shook her. She gripped the steer-
ing wheel with all her might, gasping with sobs as the
narrator on the cassette tape continued. Two decades of
rebellion were melting away like the snowpack in the
spring. The love of the Savior had touched her at last.

Darlene's mother remembers Darlene as "a very
loving and caring daughter." When she was five years
old, she was to have her tonsils removed. On the morning of the operation, Darlene began to cry as she sat with
her mother in the hospital's waiting room. While Fran
held her daughter close, Darlene said, "Mommy, you
will have to be here all by yourself while I'm gone."

At the age of fourteen, Darlene dedicated her life to
Christ. But when she turned fifteen, she began to bris-
tle at authority. Her mother placed her in a Christian
home for troubled kids, but they could not get through
to her either. There, Darlene met a rebel named Gary.
He became her first love, and stole her innocence. Fran
grieved again when a man raped Darlene, prompting
Gary to break off his relationship with her. Broken-
hearted, Darlene became callous and jaded.

"One day she was loving and caring, the next she
became abusive, unkind, and hateful, with a terrible atti-
tude," her mother said. "I'd lie in bed at night waiting
for her to come in. Then I'd get up and tell her she was
grounded, but then she wouldn't come home from
school for days. I'd phone the school only to find out

she hadn't attended classes. I'd pray with her but she would mumble hateful things under her breath. Finally, her brother, Phil, talked to her. Darlene listened, then went right out and did her own thing. When she disappeared, I was frantic. I called the police, only to be told: 'Lady, there are thousands out there on the road. There's nothing we can do."

Young and angry, Darlene hitchhiked to the Florida Keys, where she cut off ties with her family. By this time, Fran had moved to Denver. In 1968, the family put down roots in Littleton, Colorado. Proud of her exploits, Darlene occasionally shared bits and pieces of news with one or another of her loved ones. She used LSD, mescaline, and marijuana. She took hallucinogenic mushrooms, barbiturates, quaaludes, methedrine, and cocaine—whatever gave her a buzz in her reckless pursuit of pleasure. Her family looked on helplessly as she became addicted to heroin. Without warning, Darlene would pop into her mother's home in Littleton. The shock would nearly destroy Fran, and then she would try to clean her up, buy her some new clothes, and get her to eat some good food.

As time went by, the family began to see Darlene more. When they could arrange a reunion, the family had fun—but the language out of her mouth "would curl your hair," her mother said. Diane would tell her sister to watch her mouth, but it was pointless. Fran kept praying, holding on to the biblical promise, "Train up a child in the way he should go, and when he is old he will not depart from it." Darlene's mother prayed for thirty years. When Diane would ask, "Mom, what are we going to do about her mouth?" Fran would reply, "Honey, let's be patient. She's been talking that way for most of her adult life. We can't expect too much."

At some point Darlene began to reap the blessings of her mother's faithful prayers. Her life began to stabilize a bit, and she married a man named Mike and moved with him to Glenwood Springs. In 1986, Diane moved back to Colorado and discovered that her sister had organized the M & D Cleaning Service, a specialty housecleaning service that took care of private homes nestled among the ski resorts of Western Colorado. Living closer allowed the sisters to visit more often.

Then in 1996, Darlene was injured so badly in an automobile accident that she was forced to drive to Denver a couple of times a month to see physicians. "Our relationship grew into something much more precious," Diane recalls. "Mom and I enjoyed spending quality time with Darlene. Always the conversations would turn to the spiritual." When Diane suggested that God might be "trying to get your attention but maybe you haven't been listening," Darlene did not disagree. "Sometimes God has to tear a person down in order to finally start building them back up again and make them whole," Diane said.

From then until October 2000 their dialogue progressed until Darlene listened to the Left Behind tapes and surrendered her heart to God. Back home in

Glenwood Springs, Darlene called her mother and sister and, through her tears, gave a full account of her return to God.

"She came to see us on December 2, alone without Mike," Diane recalled, "and my—*what a difference!* No cussing, no drinking. . . . We went to two Christmas concerts and to church on Sunday morning. Darlene cried through the worship service and both concerts. Darlene is our Christmas miracle." At first, Mike was furious about her conversion, but he later acknowledged that she had done the right thing.

Darlene had been baptized as a child, but when she told her mother, "I would like to be baptized again as a testimony to my new life," her mother said, "Honey, go for it!" Her brother and sisters and uncles and aunts were all present to witness the miracle.

After her conversion, Darlene asked her mother not to bother getting her the rest of the Left Behind cassettes. She'd already gone out and bought them all.

Diane read all the books in the Left Behind series, too. Now that her sister is back in the fold, "He can return at any time," she says.

Darlene agrees. It's hard to attend church without her husband, but on Mother's Day 2002 he gave her a card and a plant. "It was a prayer answered," Darlene told her family. This prayer expresses her gratitude:

> God my Father, Lord my Savior, I thank You for all
> Your love that You have given me, not only now

but also in the past. I had asked You into my life when I was young, then turned my back on You for so many years. But during those years You were always by my side, especially in my darkest hour. I didn't know it then, but I do now as You hold me in Your arms and keep me alive. I owe all that I have to Jesus, who died for me. Thank You for bringing me home again, that I may worship You. The love, joy, peace, and calm I have could come only from You. I love You with all my heart and soul. They shall be Yours forever. In Your most precious name, amen.

"Please continue writing even after the 'Glorious Appearing' takes place. Tell us about their first year in heaven—what they will see, what they will do . . . I'm so excited!"

—LORI E.

"While reading the first book, I almost cried because I know what many of my friends will have to go through. I need to witness to my friends, knowing there will be someone like Carpathia who tricks people and gets away with murder."

—KILYNN S.

"My daughter suggested that I read *Left Behind,* because all her friends are reading it. I felt the anointing of the Holy Spirit while reading. I don't see it as fiction. This entire series should be passed down from generation to generation."

—V. P. WASHINGTON

"Stories don't get any better than *Left Behind.* The way these books are written, I become any character I want to every time I open the book. They send a powerful message. You are definite inspirations to Christian writers everywhere, and a definite inspiration to me. You've shown me that I should write about what I was put on this earth to write about."

—HEATHER H.

IF . . .

━━━━━━━━━━━━━━━━━━━━━━━━━━━━━━━

WHATEVER IS IN YOUR

HEART DETERMINES

WHAT YOU SAY.

— MATTHEW 12:34

Christmas lights brightened Cartersville, Georgia, for the 1998 holidays as Lori Lee Sanders popped into her parents' house on an errand. "Lori," her mother, Linda, said as her daughter was leaving, "here's a book I'd like you to read. You'll enjoy it."

"Thanks," Lori said, glancing at the title, but she was thinking, *No way am I going to put aside my romance novels for a religious book.*

On the short trip home to prepare dinner for her

husband, Woody, and their two sons, Joshua and Caleb, Lori peeked at *Left Behind*. She flipped open its cover, and her suspicions were confirmed. She carried it into the house, tossed it on the nightstand beside her bed, and forgot it.

Life was stressful at the Sanders household, and morning was sometimes the worst of all. Lori would yell and Woody would argue with her. Then he would slam the front door on his way out to work. Joshua and Caleb would sit in the family room trying to stay invisible to avoid the notice of their angry father. Lori would hide in her own way, taking a tranquilizer as she slipped on her Nikes for her daily six-mile run.

Neither Lori nor Woody had any interest in the Bible, or in having a morning quiet time, although Lori had seen her parents do it many times while she was growing up on the mission field. She had prayed the sinner's prayer of repentance at the age of five. "I always told people I was a Christian," she said. "I could say 'God' but I was embarrassed to say 'Jesus.' " Woody had long forgotten the catechism of the Presbyterian church in which he'd been reared. To him, the Bible was a black book full of dull stories about ancient people, with no relevance to life today.

Lori had more immediate concerns, like the fear of gaining weight. After avoiding food for two days she would fix herself meals of V8 juice, apples, crackers, diet Cokes, gum, and hard candy. If her stomach was full, she felt fat. On weekends she would "pig out" on junk food—chocolate bars, pizza, donuts, and other fattening foods. To punish herself, she would then exercise desperately. For seventeen years, she bounced like a yo-yo between eating and fasting as she whipped her body in a vicious cycle of vengeance.

Then there was her deteriorating marriage. Hopelessness, fear, and loneliness ruled the Sanders home. How had everything degenerated into such a mess? Why couldn't a marriage counselor help? Why were the fights with Woody growing increasingly bitter? Why were the boys afraid of their dad and jittery at school?

"I was emotionally, physically, and mentally bankrupt that night in mid-January 1999 when I picked up *Left Behind* and started to read," Lori said. "Little did I know that God was patiently bringing me to the point of surrender."

About fifty pages into the book, Lori asked herself, *If the Rapture happened right now, would I go to heaven? Well, if I didn't go up in the Rapture, would I get a second chance during the Tribulation? But if I die before the Rapture, then what?*

Suddenly Lori heard a voice in her mind saying, "You are straddling a fence. You say you are a Christian, but you don't act or live like one." She placed *Left Behind* facedown on the couch, fell to her knees, and began to weep. Through her tears, for the first time in her life, she saw the horror of her sins in the light of the Lord's holiness.

"Then and there I met my Lord and Savior, Jesus

Christ," she said. "My heart became His. He washed me clean, poured out His mercy and grace, gave me His peace, and filled my once-empty heart with His inexpressible joy. It was like nothing I had ever known."

The next morning was wonderful. "I felt *alive*. I could hardly wait to tell my parents what had happened."

The minute their daughter walked into their house that morning, Doug and Linda Cozart knew that something wonderful had happened, because "her feet hardly touched the floor."

But Woody was not as thrilled. He was confused by the change in his wife. When Lori explained what had happened, he cut her off impatiently. "Yeah, well, we shall see if you can walk the talk." *Here we go again*, he thought. *She'll be obsessed for a while and then she'll quit and move on to something else.*

Lori insisted that she was a different person. One proof was that she did not yell back at him when his ugly barbs pricked her senses. She wanted desperately for her husband to know Jesus, too.

That evening when Woody burst through the door and began to verbally abuse his family, Lori heard the Holy Spirit urging her: *Go put your arms around him.* She obeyed and they were both shocked by what happened. Lori felt warm all over, and a gentleness toward Woody that she had not experienced in years. They began laughing together. They discussed issues of the day instead of arguing about them.

When Lori wanted to attend church and take the boys with her, Woody didn't object. Ten days later, as his wife and sons were dressing for church, Woody announced that he was going with them.

"My shoes look okay?" he asked.

"Yes!" she said as Woody pulled her into a fierce embrace.

Through tears, Woody asked Lori to forgive him for being such an angry husband. He went to each son and apologized for the way he had treated him. His marriage was resurrected that morning and has never been more alive.

Habitual profanity ceased. Lori's tranquilizers and painkillers went down the drain at the kitchen sink. She started eating balanced meals again, threw out all her secular music, and replaced her romance novels with one inspiring book after another.

"The thing that makes it most exciting," Lori said, "is the Bible. For the first time in my life I have a desire to read it—and I *understand it!* Suddenly, John the Baptist, and the apostles Peter, Paul, and John are real people instead of merely names. And best of all, Jesus, my wonderful Savior, is alive. He is the head of our home. I recognize His voice as I read His precious Word."

As much as Lori loves to read the Bible, she enjoys teaching it even more. About her college degree in secondary education she jokes, "I was half right. Teaching high school social studies was not the career God had planned for me. Instead, he gave me the gift of teaching His Word. He has opened the door for me to teach the sixth and twelfth grade girls' Sunday school classes at our church. My greatest desire is for the Holy Spirit to speak through me, to show the girls how the Bible relates to their lives."

Woody's faith has continued to deepen too after his "life-changing commitment," as evidenced by his deep hunger for intimacy with the Father. Now Woody also teaches a young men's Sunday school class and is a member of the pastor's discipleship group taught monthly at the church.

"What amazes me in all this," says Woody, "is God's sovereignty. He guided my steps before I made Jesus my Savior and Lord."

If Linda Cozart hadn't given her daughter *Left Behind* . . .

If Lori hadn't read it . . .

If . . .

"I know, I know—it's fiction. But after reading the series, I was so profoundly influenced by the basis of it that I was led to be saved after forty-seven aimless, wasted years on this earth. I was told in church last Sunday that there's 'no second chance.' I'm starting to read the Bible for myself."

—DONNY H.

"Before *Left Behind,* my life was a never-ending parade of confusion with no way to make a choice that included Jesus. Now I turn all of my concerns about my family over to Christ. He shows me the way."

—DENNIS G.

"You have changed this person's life! There are no words to express my thankfulness! I pray for you every night in your quest to share Christ with the world."

—EMILY JANE J.

"I have tried for years to understand the Bible and have lost the battle. I've asked questions of priests, nuns, and deacons and gotten the same answer: "Go read your Bible." So I gave up, until I spotted *Left Behind* at Sam's Club. Couldn't put it down! Read it three times with the Bible close by, looking up everything. Suddenly everything clicked. Can't stop studying!

—MARCIA A.

CAN GOD
FORGIVE ME?

FRIENDS SHARE

ALL THINGS.

—PYTHAGORAS

Bruce and Yvonne Dahlstrom of Riverside, California, consider themselves to be an "average American couple." He is a hard-working farm boy from Wisconsin who is now self-employed selling commercial refrigeration and air-conditioning. Yvonne was raised in California and is now a mother of two. Their son, Mitchell, a bighearted fellow with artistic ability, loves kids. His sister, Erika, is three years younger. She's a fun-loving but studious young lady who gets good grades in school, displays a mature sense of humor, and frequently invites neighborhood kids to enjoy the family swimming pool.

Bruce and Yvonne agreed at the start of their marriage that they would say "I love you" to each other every day—and mean it. Why, then, as her husband expressed his love so generously, did Yvonne find herself becoming more and more unhappy? Where did her anger—the taking of the Lord's name in vain, her impatience at the slightest delay—come from?

"In all honesty," she said, "I began cussing like a sailor. Beautiful house, great husband, healthy kids— and yet I was becoming more and more angry and depressed."

She cried uncontrollably, feeling empty and unfulfilled, and slept many an afternoon away, caught in emotional doldrums. Bruce, unable to help, would hold her and hope for a change.

The Dahlstroms found a small church close by and began attending as a family. A neighbor named Joani, who attended the same church, stopped by one afternoon to share a book she had enjoyed. The title, *Left Behind*, intrigued Yvonne. The flyleaf said that the story had to do with the Bible and about events in the end times—something Yvonne had always been curious about.

One night, unable to sleep, she went downstairs, sat on the couch, and began reading the novel. As she read, the story took hold of her. When she read about the Rapture that would snatch believers out of the world, it felt as if the messages were written directly to her. When the main character, Rayford Steele, tried unsuccessfully to find answers in the Bible, Yvonne exclaimed, "That's me!" Like Steele, she had tried several times to read and understand the Bible, but could not comprehend its message. It was, to Yvonne, "pure gibberish."

How can people read this stuff and understand it? she often wondered.

Yvonne knew nothing about God and what he required of her, but somehow she yearned to be good enough to earn the right to enter Heaven to spend eternity with him.

When she reached page 200 in the novel, there it was—as if spoken directly to her—an exhortation for new believers by the fictional young pastor who had not been taken up in the Rapture. Then, on page 209, the scene depicted a videotape with a message from the church's former pastor—who *had* been taken up in the Rapture—that carried the Bible's message of hope: "The sting of death is sin, and the strength of sin is the law. But thanks be to God, who gives us victory through our Lord Jesus Christ."

Yvonne stiffened. Suddenly she saw herself as God sees her—a sinner with a fallen nature, unable to be good enough or do enough worthy acts to earn her way into heaven. She continued reading until page 215. Halfway down the page she read,

> *If you accept God's message of salvation, his Holy*
> *Spirit will come in unto you and make you spiritually*

*born anew. You don't need to understand all this theo-
logically. You can become a child of God by praying to
him right now. . . .*

"I slid to my knees as the airline captain had done,"
Yvonne recalled, "and I bawled. I recited the prayer of
salvation, then sat back on the sofa and tried to make
sense of the joy and peace that was suddenly filling my
mind."

A clock chimed 2 A.M. Renewed and exhilarated,
Yvonne climbed the stairs, crawled into bed, and had
the most peaceful night's rest she'd enjoyed in months.

That Sunday, Yvonne told her husband, "If the
pastor asks who wants to receive Jesus into their lives,
I'm going forward."

Bruce shrugged. "Okay," he said.

Yvonne sat next to her friend Joani and whispered
to her the same thing she had told her husband. No
altar call was given, but after the service, she approached
Pastor Van Dine and asked him to lead her in a prayer,
mistakenly thinking that she had to be coached by a
clergyman before redemption could take effect.

Later Yvonne realized, "God had met me there in
my home at two o'clock in the morning when I called
out to him. And he used the *Left Behind* novel to reach
me. I was born again. The date was March 16, 2000."

Yvonne now sat often at her kitchen table, reading
her new Bible. She started at the beginning and was
amazed by her ability to understand. She "no longer felt

empty. Jesus filled that spot. I discarded my baggage through Jesus' forgiveness and each day I watch in excitement to see how God is going to bring all of our family and friends to Himself."

Mitchell and Erika have since committed their lives to Christ, too. All three are praying for Bruce, who "still needs to be persuaded and convinced that there really is a God." His name is at the top of Yvonne's "salvation prayer list," just as the fictional Irene had her husband, Rayford, at the top of hers.

"It's amazing how one leap of faith can change your entire life forever," Yvonne said. "Jesus has put my life right side up. There aren't enough words to express how grateful I am that God can love and accept a sinner like me."

"I am tested daily. I have lost my insurance coverage and cannot afford medication for my never-ending pain. Just when I thought I couldn't stand it any longer, I found a gift card to Kmart that I had forgotten about. At Kmart, your books were on display, so I got my prescription filled with part of the gift-card money, and bought a book with the rest. To me, your books are the best medicine in the world."

—JANE D.

"The Left Behind: The Kids series is a wonderful tool for parents who want to open a discussion of Christianity with their children but haven't found a way to communicate their beliefs in a way children can understand. The adult series communicates with adults who may not be members of a church, or those who find the book of Revelation too cryptic or too far removed from our everyday lives."

—CURRIE S.

"I worried I would go crazy waiting for *Assassins* to come out so I slowed my pace to a chapter a week. That was tedious. Honestly, these books changed my life for the better and have strengthened my faith."

—CODY L.

A CRY IN
THE NIGHT

COME QUICKLY, MY LOVE!

—SONG OF SONGS 8:14

Strains of Lohengrin's "Wedding March"
wafted to the vaulted ceiling of the Immaculate Concep-
tion Church in Chicago as Diane took a deep breath and
began her walk down the flower-lined aisle of the vener-
able sanctuary. On that summer day in 1968, "Big Mike"
eagerly pledged his troth, "for better or for worse," to the
lady of his dreams. After their prom night when they
were seventeen, there had never been any thought of
anyone else.

Mike, who had been raised in a loving home,
settled with his bride in a small house in Evergreen
Park, a Chicago suburb, and plunged into his work as

a machinist. Over the next several years, they had two daughters and a son, and Mike's job allowed them a comfortable life. Diane often cooked Mike's favorite dish—ham dumplings, her Lithuanian specialty—and always had dinner ready when he got home from work. Mike loved to roll on the floor with his youngsters during the evening, play hide and seek, build with Legos, or read the kids a book.

Why, then, did Mike always feel a measure of discontent—that there had to be more to life than the blessings of a good wife, a healthy family, and a good job? What pulled him away to start spending evenings with some of his wild, single buddies? Why did his relationship with Diane begin to grow distant, when she was as good to him as a wife could be? How could his loving daughters and adoring son come to mean so little to him? How did everything good that he had fail to keep him from drifting into the arms of a stranger?

When Mike told Diane that he no longer loved her and wanted out of the marriage, she was completely blindsided. She cried for hours as her children tried to stop her tears, their little hands and arms reaching out to comfort her, their tearful kisses covering her cheeks.

Mike was angry and resentful. "I never have fun anymore," he complained. "You expect me to endure that racket at work all day and then come home and just *sit*? Look, I'm not getting any younger." After thirteen years of marriage, Mike had chosen a different life, a life that didn't include Diane or the children.

The days ahead were difficult for Diane, with no husband, no father to help with the children, and no breadwinner bringing home money for food and the mortgage. Mike sent no alimony or child support. She was able to find jobs that allowed her to be at home for her kids after school, but they paid her only minimum wage. Her skills had suffered after being unemployed for eight years, and the job market at that time was in recession. To make ends meet, Diane took in sewing jobs and worked as a baby-sitter.

After Diane went to court, sporadic payments from Mike appeared. When these eventually dried up, a second judge decreed that Mike's wages were to be garnished for monthly child support. Whatever measure of love and respect his children still held for him had dwindled. When news came that Mike had married his mistress, all of Diane's hope for reconciliation vanished.

In 1987, she ventured into a second marriage. Together they purchased a beautiful house and she started to rebuild a family. Unfortunately, her new husband was an alcoholic. In his frequent drunken rages, he began to resent Diane and her children. The promises made at the altar to love, honor, and cherish Diane were forgotten, and their house never became a home. After seven long years, Diane was again in divorce court. She prayed desperately, "I can't handle another crisis, God."

As she searched for the peace that her heart ached

to know, she looked in the wrong places. Her search led her to investigate New Age spirituality, and she became hooked. Still, something important was missing. What was it?

In 1997, sixteen years after her divorce from Mike, Diane began receiving calls from him. His voice sounded tired and distant. "My wife makes me miserable," he said. "I'm so lonely. I realize now what I did to you and what I threw away." He begged Diane to forgive him. "I forgave you a long time ago," Diane assured him.

His last and longest call to Diane came in late June that year. Then the phone stopped ringing. Diane later learned that one day Mike had sat down on the sofa in his beautiful home by the side of a private lake, put a loaded pistol to his head, and pulled the trigger.

When Diane and the children heard about Mike's death, they mourned him. Although they had not seen him for many years, the kids remembered all the wonderful things they had shared with their dad when they were younger. Diane mourned him by remembering the joys she had once known and all the things that now could never be because Mike had been unable to find enough resolve, peace, restoration, and love to live. In her need and loneliness, Diane continued to pursue New Age formulas for comfort and a measure of hope for her future. During a coffee break at work, the sales manager noticed that she was reading *Conversations with God*, a New Age book. He asked her if she had ever heard of a book entitled *Left Behind*.

"Not interested," she told him bluntly. "But I have a book I'd like *you* to read."

Her coworker took a sip of coffee, thought a moment, then suggested, "Tell you what. You read *Left Behind* and I'll read your New Age book."

Diane grudgingly agreed. But after finishing *Left Behind*, she said, "I couldn't wait to get the second book in the series. But I didn't want to act too eager. I wasn't convinced yet." One by one, she began to work her way through the Left Behind series. As she read, she learned that the Bible is not merely a book of rules but also of promises—and of news about a loving God who has provided salvation for rebellious sinners. She knew in her heart that Jesus was her Savior, but she was afraid to commit.

Diane had recently finished reading *Apollyon*, book number five in the twelve book series, when the terrorists crashed jetliners into the World Trade Center and the Pentagon. The vivid portrayals of stories about the Apocalypse caused her to consider her accountability to God. "I caught a glimpse of what's going to happen in the future," she said.

As she sat in her favorite chair one evening, she looked for a long time at the Bible in her hands. Then she took a deep breath, opened it to the first verse of the first chapter in the first book, and began reading Genesis 1:1—"In the beginning God created the heavens and the earth."

As she read day by day, peace settled upon her soul.

The God of Abraham, Isaac, and Jacob stirred her heart. As she read the New Testament, Christ became her Savior. She placed her trust in the Man of Galilee and His Kingdom.

For Diane, life made a 180-degree turn toward real hope when she read *Left Behind*. In the spring of 2002, she was baptized and joined the fellowship of believers at nearby Hope Community Church. God had answered her cry.

"A radio station in Milwaukee says that if you can't find the words to help turn someone's life around, just give them a copy of *Left Behind*. I've done it! And I've turned a few around."

—ANGELMOM

"Since my two sons and I started reading your books, we've been attending a wonderful church. We have all been saved, and the three of us were baptized this past summer. We're praying for my husband to receive the Lord. He's reading, so we know Jesus is knocking at his heart's door."

—CHERYL G.

"I've been a Christian since I was seven, but I haven't behaved like one for years. Thanks to your books, I have reconfirmed my life to God. Despite many hardships, I refused to turn my life over to God—until two weeks ago! Now I no longer worry. I know he will take care of me and my children. I know he will provide for us."

—CHERYLL D.

A TRUCKER'S PRAYER

AND NOW, ALL GLORY TO GOD,

WHO IS ABLE TO KEEP YOU

FROM STUMBLING.

—JUDE 24

Guy Archer wrestled his green eighteen-wheel Freightliner tanker truck off the loading tarmac at the Cargill Company in Dayton, Ohio and headed west on Route 70 toward Indianapolis. A sliver of sunrise in the eastern sky was reflected in his rearview mirrors and illuminated a box of four cassette tapes of the book *Left Behind* sitting on the seat beside him, a present from his girlfriend, Linda.

"Someday, people just like us," she had said,

"going about their normal routines, will suddenly vanish, and those left behind will wonder what happened."

Crazy, thought Guy as he shifted gears to begin an uphill stretch toward Englewood. At the top of the rise, he engaged the cruising gear and settled back for the two-hour run. By noon, the 52,000 pounds of corn syrup in his shiny silver tanker would be delivered to the laboratories of the Eli Lilly Company in Indianapolis. There, technicians would feed the enzymes, kill them, and then extract insulin to package as medicine for diabetics. *Quite an improvement,* Guy thought, *over the old days when they had to process hog pancreases to get insulin.*

At Richmond, he reached over, grabbed the packet of cassettes, and tossed them into the glove box. "Later, 'gator."

The morning radio talk shows touched on the usual frivolous topics. The longer Guy listened, the more his mind wandered. He thought of Linda's words: "Mass confusion will grip the world. Then a dangerous man will rise up from the confusion with the 'answers' to what's going on. . . ."

With a shrug, Guy opened the glove box. He selected the first cassette, slipped it into the tape deck, and leaned back to listen.

Rayford Steele's mind was on a woman he had never touched. With his fully loaded 747 on autopilot above the Atlantic en route to a 6 A.M. landing at Heathrow . . .

Guy braked for a station wagon that cut in front of him, then ran through the gears until his rig was at full speed again.

God was okay with Rayford Steele. But since Irene had hooked up with a smaller congregation and was into weekly Bible studies and church every Sunday, . . .

Guy thought again of his girlfriend, beautiful Linda Gail, back in Dayton at her hairdressing salon. "I love you," she had told him last night. "It hurts me to think that you would be left on earth to endure 'the time of Jacob's trouble.' " The trucker leaned over the wheel and turned up the volume of the cassette:

. . . If only Irene hadn't gone off on this new kick. Would it fade—her preoccupation with the end of the world, with the love of Jesus, with the salvation of souls? Lately she had been reading everything she could get her hands on about the Rapture of the church. "Can you imagine, Rafe," she exulted, "Jesus coming back to get us before we die?"

"Yeah, boy," he said, peeking over the top of his newspaper, "that would kill me."

She was not amused. "If I didn't know what would happen to me," she said, "I wouldn't be glib about it."

"I do know what would happen to me," he insisted. "I'd be dead, gone, finis. But you, of course, would fly right up to heaven."

As the narrative continued above the droning of the Freightliner's diesel engine, Guy again pictured Linda's sweet face, felt her grip on his arm, and heard her warning: "There will be mass confusion around the world, Guy. Then a man will rise up from the confusion. . . . "

Now the story began to make clear the Bible's message of the end times. There was no biblical promise that assured Guy of another day to live, no promise that the coming of Christ would be delayed one moment longer.

Back at the Stylish Lines hair salon, Linda was praying for Guy. Guy had all the qualities of the husband she had prayed for, except for his lack of a strong belief in God. The only issue left unsettled in their relationship was the most important one: He had never opened his heart to receive Christ as his Savior. Guy Archer would be left behind at the Rapture.

That afternoon, as Guy drove the now-empty tanker toward home, he continued to listen to the tapes of *Left Behind*. A curious resolve began to rise in his heart not to postpone the decision one more day. The words of a hymn he had heard long ago began to ring in his mind: *What a friend we have in Jesus, all our sins and griefs to bear.* He began to focus on the eternal choice before him. The thought of turning his back on the Savior's love, of never seeing Linda again, of eternal punishment, of passing through "Jacob's trouble"—all this pulled on his heart to accept God's gift without delay.

There wouldn't be much help from his mother or father. His father had been reared in a Methodist home, but had never spoken to Guy or his brother about faith in God. His mother had turned to yoga and New Age for "fulfillment." Had she ever even *heard* of Christ's second coming?

Back in Dayton, he parked his empty tanker in a grocery store lot, filled out his logbook, and pitched it into his briefcase. He thought about the day five months ago, at the end of a bad relationship, when he had pulled out the Bible his grandmother had given him for high school graduation. He had placed it on a chair and knelt beside it. "God, all I want is the right thing to happen," he had prayed. Now he felt that the right thing *was* happening, in answer to his prayer.

He phoned Linda.

"Let's drive down to talk to my cousin Lester," she suggested. "He's a pastor."

The angels sang that evening as twenty-eight-year-old Guy Archer knelt at the altar and prayed the sinner's prayer for salvation. He felt a kinship with Captain Rayford Steele, but was thankful he hadn't been left behind. Exactly one month later, on March 5, 1999, Guy was baptized and joined Cornerstone Baptist Temple in Dayton, where he is an active member and substitute bus driver.

On December 11, 1999, Guy and Linda were married.

At the dinner table recently, Guy read the words of

the apostle Paul in 1 Corinthians 15:51, just as the fictional pastor Vernon Billings had read them at New Hope Village Church in Mount Prospect, Illinois: "Behold, I tell you a mystery. We shall not all sleep, but we shall all be changed." He and Linda smiled, and then Guy thanked the Lord Jesus Christ that neither he nor his wife will be left behind when the roll is called up yonder.

You may still see Guy's green Freightliner, its silver tank streaking through the dawn, hauling corn syrup to laboratories and food factories. The insulin produced still gives health to diabetics, but now the faith in Guy's heart gives the promise of eternal life to him and to everyone who calls upon the name of Christ for salvation.

"I found Jesus Christ today after being a Wiccan for six years, caught in a trap that claimed to find a higher spirituality, but concerning itself only with this earth. I thank him because I sure don't deserve His grace. A part of my journey was reading the Left Behind books. Was it the warnings of impending doom for sinners? Special friends . . . your books . . . the New Testament . . . and now, well, my old life is shed. I'm born anew."

—JAMES S.

"I was skeptical. What could I get out of *fiction* to learn about God—especially since I was already searching for truth? So . . . I read two chapters, then started *devouring* the book. Then came the surprise. Through a fictional portrayal of a prophesied event, I found truth. Light came back into my life, illuminating and burning inside. I had never felt this way before. I *needed* God! I *wanted* him. Sure, I can *say* I believe, but I really need to *show* it. You may have thought you were simply putting true Bible passages into a fictional web. You were actually helping the Almighty to change lives—including mine!"

—AMANDA P.

GOD WAS POUNDING ON MY DOOR

INDEED, GOD IS READY

TO HELP YOU RIGHT NOW.

TODAY IS THE DAY

OF SALVATION.

—2 CORINTHIANS 6:2

Jessica Cheyenne Beavers worked nights at the public library, refilling the shelves with returned books. She was a student at Illinois College, a small liberal arts school in central Illinois. She loved the feel of books, reading snatches of some, and checking out others to enjoy at home. Because her father was in the air force, Jessica and her family had lived in five states, as well as in Japan and Italy.

In the late 1990s, Jessica noticed more and more visitors checking out a book in the fiction section titled *Left Behind*. At the time, only six of the twelve books slated for the series were in print, and the library ordered all of them: *Left Behind, Tribulation Force, Nicolae, Soul Harvest, Apollyon,* and *Assassins.*

Religion wasn't a topic discussed at the Beavers' house. Nobody thought about church. Although Jessica had decided she was an agnostic, she thought she would enjoy the story about millions of people suddenly disappearing.

As she began to read *Left Behind*, Jessica made an amazing discovery. There were people who believed that Jesus Christ was going to return to earth someday. She looked in the Bible and found the same account. Not only was He going to return, but He was going to take believers to heaven. *Believers?* she thought. *What is that? I'm going to heaven, too, right? I'm not all that bad. I'm not a murderer, and I try to help everyone I can.*

Jessica had to find out the truth, but how? *Church! Of course.* Her boyfriend, Greg, had spoken to her about attending The Way Home Church, so she decided to tag along with him the very next Sunday. What she heard astounded her. She thought that church was supposed to be boring. But these people were happy, excited about the Bible and all that it had to say to believers today. They sang together, prayed together, listened to the pastor explain passages of hope from the Bible, and were knit together into a loving fellowship. Jessica felt foolish, not knowing the simplest answers to basic questions.

Back home, not long after her first visit to The Way Home Church, Jessica had a vision. "I was frightened," she said, wondering at the sudden intrusion of the unknown. "Suddenly, I was at a music festival in a prayer tent in an open field asking the questions I hadn't had the courage to ask before. And I was crying because I had just done something very important and meaningful."

Later, when Greg told her about the Cornerstone Festival, a weeklong festival of music, prayer, and worship in Bushnell, Illinois, a light went on. Jessica began working on her mother to let her attend. "I couldn't tell my mother about the vision," she said, "or about *Left Behind,* so it took some time and a lot of work to talk her into the idea. But I absolutely *had* to go."

Finally, permission came to attend the midsummer open-air festival. Jessica and Greg traveled the seventy-seven miles to Bushnell with friends. After staking out a campsite in an open field, with blankets, ice chests and a small tent, Jessica and her group settled down to enjoy the program.

At the end of each day, seekers crowded into a prayer tent, but Jessica was afraid, so she put off going to the tent herself. Then, on the second-to-last night, she and Greg and a couple of the other guys attended a concert given by the O. C. Supertones. Jessica stood on the fringes of the crowd, listening. Suddenly a band member began to pray, and then he led the crowd in singing and in worship. Some people raised their hands in supplication to heaven.

"I cried as I watched this and realized that I wanted to be a part of this, the body of Christ," Jessica said. "God was pounding on my door. I did not want to be left behind when the Savior came for His family of redeemed people, but I was still too frightened to step out."

She finished the concert in tears, feeling love and acceptance radiating from the crowd of Christians.

The next morning, she awoke determined to get to the prayer tent at all costs. One of the guys in her group decided to move his car so he could get out easily after the final concert to start home. As he drove down an embankment of soft dirt, his car became stuck, so he recruited several strong men to help push it out. Jessica was standing nearby as the car began to move. "Watch your feet!" someone yelled to her, but it was too late. The right rear tire ran over her foot, pressing it hard into the oozing mud. It hurt a lot, but there didn't seem to be anything broken. Still, with her foot aching so much, it just wasn't going to be possible to walk all the way over to the prayer tent.

"The trip seemed to be in vain," Jessica recalled. "Maybe I hadn't had a vision at all. Maybe it was just a dream. I had deliberately put off making any decision, yet that entire week opened my eyes and heart. It was now or never."

"As we neared my house, I asked Greg to pull over to the side of the road. 'God wants me to pray,' I told him. And I felt he wanted this man I loved to lead me in the sinner's prayer."

On a humid summer night in central Illinois, Jessica cried as she prayed, confessing to God that she was a sinner. Then she reached out by faith to Jesus, who had died for her sins on the cross. After she prayed, Jessica hugged Greg. The dashboard clock read 12:05 A.M. on July 8, 2001. It marked the first day of her salvation. She rested confidently in the promise of God that she would not be left behind when the Lord comes and the Antichrist is set loose.

"My life is different and I love it," she said. "I now read the Left Behind books with confidence that I won't be left behind. I worry less, I care more, and I have found the perfect church for me. The Way Home Church meets every Sunday at some member's house. We are a small group, but the Bible says in Matthew 18:20: 'Where two or three gather together because they are mine, I am there among them.'"

"I gave my father one of the Left Behind books for Christmas. This is the first time he has read a book we've given him. He is asking many questions, and we see the Holy Spirit at work in his heart. He may be close to repentance."

—JOY M.

"I *thought* I was a Christian. Like Bruce, the pastor in the story, I'd been playing. Thank you for the wake-up call. *Left Behind* has changed my life. It's touched many in my family, and we are hoping to touch more.

—JAN E.

"I had problems with depression, anxiety, and panic attacks. . . . My husband and I were on the verge of divorce. I felt alone and lost, just incomplete. I read your books, prayed the sinner's prayer, and have been filled with the Holy Spirit. My marriage has turned around; my husband and I are like newlyweds. Our six-year-old child is much happier. Tears are rolling down my cheeks. I'm so incredibly happy knowing I'll spend eternity with our heavenly Father."

—LISA L.

A COOL
DISCOVERY IN
WARM SPRINGS

IT IS NO FAULT OF

CHRISTIANITY THAT A

HYPOCRITE FALLS INTO SIN.

—ST. JEROME

Traffic was heavy on the roads leading out of Atlanta that day, but by blowing her horn and bluffing, Christine Hill managed to make progress driving her teenage son home from a private school in the city. Her shift the evening before as a waitress at Chili's had left her tired and angry.

"I could feel Stuart's eyes studying me as I honked my horn, addressed other drivers unkindly, and fought to gain a few feet on southbound 85 toward our home in Peachtree City," she said. Suddenly her son spoke up, "Mom, I wish you were a Christian."

"Wha— why Stuart, I *am* a Christian," she said. "What do you mean?"

"No, Mom," he said. "I wish you were a *real* Christian."

Hadn't her parents insisted that each kid in the family be baptized and confirmed? What more did God want? Christine's defense was hollow, and they both knew it.

A few days later, her sister hit her with another broadside. "I wish you would find God," she said. Her sister attended a Baptist church near Atlanta and enjoyed a source of peace and joy that Christine had never known. When her sister's pastor made a courtesy telephone call shortly afterward, Christine mumbled something respectable into the phone, but secretly she was wishing he would bug off.

They didn't leave her alone, however, and soon she found herself sitting one Sunday morning in the sanctuary of the Baptist church. The music was excellent and the setting so peaceful that she was completely absorbed. It was glorious.

Christine's mother owned a small specialty bookstore in Warm Springs, Georgia. On a visit to see her, Christine found herself browsing the shelves while her mother was busy with customers. Through the course of her stay, she heard that a Christian bookstore in town was going out of business. She decided to investigate, hoping to discover some bargains for her mother's shop.

Among the books she found were volumes two, five, and seven of a series titled Left Behind. Christine knew that these best-selling novels emphasized the Bible's teaching about the last days. She had heard about them and was eager to see what made them so popular.

"Is the story true?" she asked a woman in the store.

"No," she said, "but it very well could be."

Well, that got her hooked. She *had* to find out what was going on.

"You can get *Left Behind* at Wal-Mart," her mother told her. "I tried selling them in here, but my customers just have no interest in futuristic fiction."

The nearest Wal-Mart was twenty miles away in another town, but Christine decided to make the drive.

Christine was soon reading *Left Behind* and discovering things she never knew were in the Bible. What she'd heard at the Baptist church corresponded with the message of the novel. If what the pastor was saying from the pulpit was true, and if the events depicted in *Left Behind* could actually happen, Christine knew she was in trouble. One Sunday morning, she mouthed the words emblazoned across the front of the church: "Jesus did all He could for you. Will you do all you can for Him?" That would mean becoming like Irene Steele, the fictional wife in *Left Behind*, who was ready when the Lord called her home. "As a believer," Christine reasoned, "I too would be ready with my son to meet the Lord at the Rapture to be with him forever."

At home, bowing over her desk with *Left Behind* on one side and the Holy Bible on the other, Christine became a "new creature" in Christ. She had proved the words of her Lord, who said, "Keep on asking and you will be given what you ask for. Keep on looking and you will find. Keep on knocking and the door will be opened. . . . Everyone who seeks, finds. And the door is opened to everyone who knocks" (Matthew 7:7-8).

She also memorized Proverbs 4:18: "The way of the righteous is like the first gleam of dawn, which shines ever brighter until the full light of day." Joy down deep in her soul, the joy promised by her Lord, bubbled forth and changed her countenance. Now happiness fills her life. And there will be no Armageddon for her! No mark of the Beast. No fleeing the Antichrist.

One day at work, while Christine was taking orders and serving tables, a customer was watching her. "Excuse me," he said when Christine brought his check. "You're a Christian, aren't you?"

Christine stuffed her pen into her apron pocket and beamed. "Yes, I am," she said. "How'd you know?"

"I can see it in the way you treat your customers, and by your conversation. Your eyes just seem to shine with joy."

His comment reminded Christine of the words of Proverbs 4:18: "The way of the righteous . . . shines ever brighter."

"I am in the U.S. Army stationed in Korea. My wife sent me the first three books, but the third was actually the fourth, so I traveled 150 miles to the only store on the peninsula that carries the book—on an air force base, no less. Your books revived my candle. I yearn for Scripture now after being depleted and burned-out—even angry at God. Now I see that the Word of God has so much to offer.

—SGT. SHAUN M.

"How can 388 pages covering only four days be so soul-stirring and at the same time present a plot so intriguing?"

—DONNIE H.

"I work in a beauty shop and this girl came in talking about your books. So I went to the library and got one. I couldn't put it down. I went to bed . . . couldn't sleep. I'm thinking about the things that are to come. A lady at work asked me if all that was *really* in the Bible. I told her, 'Yes, it is.' I looked up everything. They have put a fire under me. I'm running a little faster for Jesus now."

—MITZI Y.

AN OILMAN'S EMPTY WELL

AND HOW DO YOU

BENEFIT IF YOU GAIN

THE WHOLE WORLD

BUT LOSE YOUR OWN

SOUL IN THE PROCESS?

—MARK 8:36

Few drivers on the Golden State Freeway noticed a Bakersfield oilman slumped in his white 1984 Ford pickup along the highway, weeping. Lee Archer, president of Archer-Reed Wireline Service, needed help. He could not have explained to anyone why he had become so discouraged, or why he was so uncertain about the future, but though he was a take-charge kind of guy, he needed the kind of help he couldn't provide for himself. A subsequent stay in a Bakersfield psychiatric ward gave him time to evaluate what was happening to his life.

Lee had enjoyed good fortune since as far back as 1959, when the veteran roustabout had $1,500, a used pickup truck, and an idea. Years of experience in the oil fields had convinced him that the industry needed an easier, faster way to service productive oil and natural gas wells. As time went on, knowledgeable industry veterans developed specialized equipment and instruments for use in the California oil fields. Soon, the aggressive use of small computers and software cut hours of field time from routine jobs. Lee Archer's company won wide acclaim as he focused on developing software-based servicing techniques. But Lee didn't realize how far his spirit of accomplishment fell short of the Spirit he needed for his soul.

Archer-Reed Wireline Service became very successful with the help of solidly loyal men and women who worked long hours and cared for their customers like family. It grew to become the largest independent company of its kind, with five offices in California and Utah. Lee spent days, then weeks, then months away from his wife, Dolly, and their two children, Kris and Brian, selling his patented invention that serviced pumping wells at a fraction of the time that manual labor required.

No husband and father is likely to remain head of his family if he is not at home. The sin of neglect, coupled with a lack of fidelity, shattered the Archer family. Lee had gained an empire while losing his marriage to divorce and sacrificing the companionship of those he loved most. When his company was sold, Lee shared the settlement with his wife, who had worked in the company from the start, and with his children. After the sale, he moved to Montana to establish a new home and later to retire. There were new business opportunities in Big Sky country, but age and failing health limited Lee's activity and left him frustrated and bored. The 1,500-mile distance between him and his kids was especially painful.

His daughter, Kris, read *Left Behind* and mailed the novel to her dad with a note urging him to read it. With almost nothing but time on his hands, Lee read the book and immediately became convicted of his need for God's forgiveness. Hoping for just such a miracle, Kris sent her father the next three books in the series. Before long, Lee Archer was examining his life, and the verdict was clear.

"When I finished reading *Left Behind*," he said, "I thought it was a great story. Successive books, however, convinced me to not only enjoy the fiction, but also to make significant changes in my personal life. It was after reading *Soul Harvest* that I made the biggest changes. That was when it became clear to me that worldly successes do not last. They had failed me when

I needed help and comfort the most. My health was poor, and my family was far away.

"*Left Behind* made it clear that all my hard work and long hours away from my home and family had brought me nothing but sorrow. I had failed to understand the reason for my existence on this earth. The depiction of the end times was key to my understanding of what's important. How could I enjoy a fulfilling relationship with anyone without first having a relationship with Christ? Without the grace that Christ provides, how could I bear the guilt of the way things should have been? The Left Behind books started me on a new journey—one that is never too late to begin."

"I read your Left Behind series, and then read them all a second time. I'm looking forward to reading them again. You have helped me to believe in God. Thank you."

—JERRY D.

"Betsy, my neighbor, begged me, 'Please don't become a fanatical Christian and don't raise your children that way, either.'

"One day her son came home and asked her how he could be saved, and what was God, and were they going to hell or not. Betsy phoned to question me. I told her, 'I must do the will of the Lord and speak the truth. I raise my children to do the same.'

"At Costco, Betsy bought *Left Behind,* and several volumes that followed, to take along on a trip. After reading the first one, she repented of her sins and asked the Lord to save her soul. As soon as she arrived home, she rushed over to tell me the good news. She is currently looking for a church home. Are these books good tools to lead unbelievers to Christ or what!"

—DEBRA T.

"Your Left Behind books have brought me back to God. I have a closer relationship with Him and am excited about worship now. I can't thank you enough."

—AMY K.

יציאת מצרים
(THE EXODUS)

LET MY PEOPLE GO.

—EXODUS 5:1

At a weekend retreat in Richmond, Virginia,
sponsored by Amway Corporation for its independent business owners, Rhonda J. Kutler decided to
visit a nondenominational church service arranged
as part of the program's activities. Raised as a
Conservative Jew, Rhonda was only vaguely aware of
what Protestants believed. She held that much of the
pain in this world was caused by religion, and she
didn't understand why people couldn't just get
along. She was suspicious of Christians but took a
seat in the chapel anyhow. Her husband, Jeff, had
convinced her that posing as a Christian was a great

way to develop a thriving business. And at age forty-four, what did she have to lose?

Soothed by the beautiful, well-played music, Rhonda also enjoyed the pastor's message of hope and eternal life—words from the Christians' end of the Bible. She thought, *Maybe the Jews don't have it together after all. Still, if all religions were eliminated from the earth, wouldn't everybody be better off?* Rhonda took stock of her life: twice divorced, not following what her parents had taught her all her life, and at war with her sister—things were not what they should have been.

She had decided early in her adult life that she had no need for religion and definitely no need for God (if God actually existed). Religions, she believed, were a bunch of rituals people followed without knowing why. Even back then she had already come to the conclusion that most of the world's pain was caused by people fighting to get other people to believe the way they do.

Rhonda had always questioned and never embraced the kosher dietary restrictions she grew up with in the Brooklyn home of her parents. She embraced Charles Darwin's theories of evolution as being "the closest thing to correct." After all, *if* God does exist, why can't we see him? Why do bad things happen to good people? She tangled with her father in heated arguments about persecution against the Jews and heard her mother refer to Christians as "those who blamed the Jews for killing Jesus."

Rhonda met her first husband while attending
Long Island University's downtown Brooklyn campus,
was married at nineteen, and divorced two years later.
She began looking for love "in all the wrong places,"
as the song goes, because she thought a man could
provide what was missing in her life. In rebellion, she
dated non-Jewish men and was married again at
twenty-seven. That explosive, abusive relationship
lasted four years, ending once again in divorce. A
couple of years later Rhonda met Jeff, but she didn't
want to get married again. Jeff felt strongly about it,
though, and wanted to "do the right thing," in accor-
dance with his Jewish upbringing. So once again
Rhonda was married. Two years later, Heather was
born. This "gift from God," as Rhonda now calls her,
became the joy of her life.

In 1996, Rhonda and Jeff joined the Amway
Corporation. Their entire lives revolved around people
and activities associated with the business. At this time,
Jeff began his pretense of acting like a Christian and of
doing Christian things such as attending church and
getting baptized. While conforming to Jeff's charade,
Rhonda actually began to draw closer and closer to
having a true relationship with Jesus.

Rhonda had begun reading *Left Behind.* The story
that unfolded was not what Rhonda had anticipated.
From its beginning, the book had her biting her finger-
nails in suspense and taking stock of her life: *Would I
be ready if Jesus came?* she thought. *No. If I died tomorrow,*

I have no idea where I'd spend eternity. With that realiza-
tion, she surrendered to the Lord.

After her conversion, she abandoned Jewish ritual
and continued attending church, and when an opportunity came to transfer Heather to a Christian school,
she took advantage of it. Jeff eventually filed for
divorce, citing Rhonda's many changes as the basis for
his filing.

Rhonda was still not 100 percent comfortable with
her newly found Christian beliefs. The traditions of her
Jewish upbringing waged war in her soul. Then in
December 1997, she made the decision to be baptized.
Fortified by what she had read in the Left Behind books,
and strengthened by her pastor's sermons at Hawthorne
Gospel Church, Rhonda's faith continued to grow
strong. "Before reading *Left Behind,*" she said, "I didn't
even know what the word *rapture* meant. Now I am truly
committed to learning about Jesus and to following in
his footsteps. I am no longer the person I once was, and
I often find myself thinking twice before doing something wrong or saying the wrong thing."

Rhonda devotes time to working as a guide with
the first grade Pioneer Girls and also serves in Sunday
School with the two-year-olds. She believes that the
younger you start instilling a love for the Lord, the
deeper the seed will root. For the past four years,
Rhonda has faithfully attended and volunteered at
Women of Faith conferences as well.

"After reading your books, the religious blindfolds over my eyes have been removed. I have taken it upon myself to make certain that more people experience this rebirth. My copies have been read by dozens of college students. Not one felt it was a waste of time."

—EDWARD J.

"I checked out *Left Behind* at our city library, while doing community service, and got hooked. The books have made me look to God."

—AMANDA B.

"Before I started reading the series, I had questions about God. The subject usually made me uncomfortable. I was confused about my beliefs and had been searching for something to give me answers about my own faith. The day I started reading *Left Behind,* I was so scared I might be left behind that it cleared up some of my own feelings and made me want to be a better Christian. Your books are the main reason why I have accepted the Lord into my life. Thanks for clearing up my questions about faith.

—SCOT W.

NO LONGER
AFRAID TO DIE

WHO ARE THOSE WHO

FEAR THE LORD? HE WILL

SHOW THEM THE PATH

THEY SHOULD CHOOSE.

—PSALM 25:12

Christian Huls of Cordova, Tennessee, laid the foundation for a happy and fulfilled life on the basis of three statements:

> "Enlightenment comes from all religions; there is no absolute truth."

"Christ's existence is a fabrication used for power
and oppression."
"Whatever I do is right, as long as it doesn't hurt
anyone else."

That perspective didn't suit his fiancée's brother-in-law,
however. He attempted to direct Christian toward the
biblical perspective on life that declares all people
sinners and asserts that Christ is the only Savior
from eternal death. Christian, however, remained
unpersuaded.

Then a serious automobile accident reminded
Christian that he was mortal and could die without
warning. Moreover, a cassette tape by Ron Carlson,
head of Christian Ministries International, confronted
him with powerful arguments against evolution. In his
refutation, Ron used the fossil record, the false ape-
men, the scientific laws of entropy and abiogenesis,
the impossibility of chance, and solid evidence that
the earth is young rather than billions of years old.

"I came to see that all those biblical stories I had
learned as a child had to be true," Christian said. "This
meant that my philosophy of life was skewed. It was
humbling."

He and his fiancée, Lee Anne, agreed they should
attend a church service. Nobody in their circle of
friends was as familiar with the Scriptures as a particu-
lar coworker of Christian's, so they agreed to visit his
church. The first result of their new pursuit was a deci-

sion to stop living together before marriage. Within two years, they had joined the church and were married.

Although their pastor mentioned the phrase "relationship with Christ," the full meaning didn't dawn on Christian and Lee Anne until much later. They had embraced Jesus Christ intellectually, but they still thought that by trying to lead a good life they could somehow become good enough to get into heaven.

One month after their wedding, Christian and Lee Anne drove past a horrifying automobile accident in which several teenagers were killed. "I had the worst feeling in the pit of my stomach as I looked at their lifeless bodies covered with tarpaulins in the street," Christian said. "I feared that if that had happened to us, I wasn't absolutely certain where I would have ended up." He still felt guilty about his past.

One evening after dinner, Christian and Lee Anne began discussing the subject of prophecy. Curious, they opened the book of Revelation and began to read. About the only thing they could understand for certain was Revelation 1:3, where Jesus promises a blessing to all who read the book.

At work the next day, Christian casually mentioned his struggles with understanding Revelation to a new employee who had mentioned in passing that she was a Southern Baptist. "Why don't you read the book *Left Behind*?" she said. "It's fiction, but it's based on events outlined in Revelation."

Christian told her that he'd seen *The Omen* and *The Seventh Sign* but thought the scripts were pretty bad. "It seems like anyone can interpret Revelation and make it mean anything they want," he said.

"I think you'll like *Left Behind*," she said. "It takes a more literal approach, beginning with the rapture of the church and continuing—"

"The *what?*" Christian interrupted. "That's not in Revelation. That's just something you Southern Baptists made up 'cause everybody makes fun of you and you can't wait to get out of here."

"Well, it's written elsewhere in the Bible too," she said..

Later, a friend showed Christian his notes from a Bible study on Revelation. He explained several ways that others interpret Revelation. However, he upheld the "futurist" viewpoint, and showed Christian why he believed the Scriptures clearly proved this was correct. This view holds that Christ will fulfill all of the prophecies of his second coming literally. He explained that whenever something in Revelation is intended to be symbolic, it is usually indicated and interpreted immediately in the context. Otherwise, it is interpreted elsewhere in Scripture. To Christian's surprise, it all made sense.

He began reading *Left Behind*, eagerly seeking answers. "If the Bible is inspired by God, wouldn't He give us something He intended us to understand?" he reasoned. He could relate to Rayford Steele, the lead

character. He could easily understand his fear that it
might be too late for salvation. Christian eagerly
followed the words quoted in a video recording by
the pastor of Rayford's church, who had left behind a
message for all: "It's not too late! Repent, and believe
the gospel."

"I've never done that—never asked Jesus to forgive
me or to come into my life," Christian said. He kept
reading. Rayford, he noted, went through a dramatic
change immediately. He began reading the Bible—not
because he thought he should but because he *wanted*
to. He began enjoying fellowship with other believers
in worship and prayer.

"Sure, I knew he was a fictional character," Christian said, "but I knew people who were just like him.
The most convicting thing to me was when something
was wrong, he would get together with other believers
and they would all get on their knees and pray
together.

"I was uncomfortable reading about that, and it
was dawning on me that something was wrong. The
ego that made me think I might help change the world
was humbled. I finally realized that I could do *nothing*
to save myself. I became broken. I desperately wanted
what Rayford had—what I knew others in my circle of
friends at church had."

Christian hesitated. He wanted to kneel by the
breakfast table right then and there, but what if his
brother-in-law, who was in the next room and not a

believer, walked in and saw him praying on his knees? He would have a big laugh.

"Suddenly I didn't care," Christian said. "I snapped the book shut, got down on my knees beside the table, and asked the Lord Jesus Christ to forgive me of my sins. I asked Him to save me. And He did!"

Christian got up from his knees transformed. He grew in his faith by leaps and bounds. A voracious hunger to know God's Word consumed him. He also read books on theology, especially those concerning prophecy. He started listening to a local Christian radio station that he couldn't stand before.

"Why are you so different?" Lee Anne asked him a week later.

Christian explained what he had done. The next day, she told him, "Last night I prayed that prayer you told me about."

They phoned Lee Anne's brother-in-law in Nashville and gave him the good news. They both wanted to be baptized in his church, because he was the one who had shown enough concern to explain biblical doctrine to them way back before they ever dreamt they would become Christians. They traveled the two hundred miles from Memphis to Donnellson Fellowship in Nashville, where Christian and Lee Anne shared with the congregation their testimonies and then were baptized. Worry over where they would land after death vanished. So did their fear of death and the emptiness that both had experienced.

En route back to Memphis, it began to snow. Cars skidded into each other right and left. Suddenly, Christian became aware that his paranoia about death had disappeared. If he died, he would go to heaven instantly. The emptiness that had gnawed at his heart had been replaced by fulfillment in Jesus.

"I found Christ at the age of forty through your books. Thank you."

—**MATTHEW B.**

"I bought the books for my daughters, but I ended up reading them myself! I thought I'd have to *make* my kids read, but I didn't. I noticed a difference in my kids after they read those blessed books."

—**FRANCHESCA K.**

"I wandered far from the path of Truth and Hope in Jesus. However, your books awakened in me a passion to search for *His* truth. Rejoice! I am not the only person to have been affected in this manner."

—**HARRY S.**

"For many years I ran from God, but my grandmother is a prayer warrior. I didn't have a chance. She introduced me to *Left Behind*. Your portrayal of character is more realistic than anything I've read."

—**JERRY P.**

PART TWO

JUST IN TIME

Today you will be with me in paradise.

Luke 23:43

A LOGGER'S FAREWELL

IF MORTALS DIE,

CAN THEY LIVE AGAIN?

—JOB 14:14

Warm breezes stirred the pines of Huckleberry Mountain north of Spokane as lumberman Tom Kennedy climbed aboard his skidder, started its diesel engine, and roared into the forest. Celebrating the arrival of spring, his younger brother Todd gave a thumbs-up as he put his noisy chain saw into the first trunk of Kennedy Lumber's claim. His brothers Troy and Tim would be along later with trucks and log chains and wedges and sledgehammers to help harvest the wood (if their dad would release them from duties on the ranch).

As he worked, big Tom counted his blessings: Jeanna, his beautiful wife . . . five spunky daughters . . . his mother and dad still in good health on the 1,800-acre family ranch just over the hill at Fruitland, eighty miles north of Spokane, where he had grown up with his three brothers and a sister—all happily married now.

Thomas Le Roy Kennedy, standing six feet three inches tall and weighing two hundred pounds, was the Irish clan's firstborn in 1961. He relished his role as elder brother on the Kennedy ranch, supervising the other four Kennedy kids: Todd, Troy, Tim, and his sister, Terri. His fierce love for his siblings was evident in how he cared for Troy, who had shattered his C-2 vertebrae in a fall while putting shingles on a roof and had to wear a "halo" apparatus for six months.

The boys grew up "picking rocks, hauling hay, and picking more rocks." Along with motorcycles, horses, and fast cars, they had cows and chickens and sold milk and eggs. They grazed sheep to keep the weeds down, but cattle and hogs were the "cash crops." The Kennedys cultivated a large vegetable garden, canned plenty for the winter, and stored potatoes in the root cellar.

Tom's dad, Gene, now had a flourishing ranch to show for all the hard work. Tom's mother, Marlene, worked as a hairdresser, but her heart was on the ranch. Tom had been diagnosed with fibromyalgia in 1990. To make matters worse, he had to watch while his formerly thriving lumber business dwindled away. The work he did as a logger kept rupturing disks in his spine. What else could he do but follow the doctor's instructions as best he could and take pain pills to keep going? The fibromyalgia was soon followed by rheumatoid arthritis. By 1997, five discs in his lower back were "blown," leaving him in constant pain during many sleepless nights. Medication became a way of life.

As the sun set on the ranch one evening in the spring of 2000, Tom's mother, Marlene, settled into her favorite chair and began reading a novel called *Left Behind*, which she had purchased after work that afternoon. She never could have imagined the impact that simple act would have on the lives of her four sons and daughter. After finishing the book, she felt an urgency to call each of her children and ask, "If you were to die today, do you know for sure you would go to heaven?"

She called Tom first. He hedged. Sure, he had been to church. He had read the Bible. But was his name written in the Lamb's Book of Life? He asked to borrow his mother's copy of *Left Behind*.

Tom finished the book quickly and responded eagerly to the call to repentance. He could talk of little else. At home, he led Jeanna and their daughters in a prayer of confession. He spoke to his brothers and sister, he phoned friends, he brought up the subject with neighbors, and told anyone who would listen about salvation through the sacrifice of God's Son on the Cross of Calvary. During a routine visit to the hospital, Tom and Jeanna listened sadly as the medical clinic's administrator gave them a familiar diagnosis: "There is nothing more we can do for you. Take these for the pain."

Tom signaled for Jeanna to follow as he headed for the door. He knew that the Demerol the doctor was prescribing would be of little help. The big man slumped into the right seat of their car as Jeanna took the wheel. Snow was falling heavier now, making their trip home treacherous. With a hurting husband beside her, Jeanna negotiated slippery Orin-Rice Road, and turned carefully onto Bentley then smashed through the snowplow's drift in front of their house, maneuvering as far up on their snowy lawn as the car would go. Tom eased himself out of the car, and Jeanna helped him safely inside the house.

Tom didn't rest long. After just two months, he signed on with a private contractor to drive a forty-ton, eighteen-wheel Kenworth tractor-trailer rig to Nashville and back, hauling freight. He spent a week getting the tractor ready and seemed eager to roll. As long as he had enough pain pills, Tom was sure he could do it.

That afternoon, with the huge truck parked in front of his house, Tom sat on the sofa with his teenage daughter Lori, listening to her frustrations about the day at school. With characteristic patience, Tom waited until she had completed her story, and then he stood up. "Well, Pete," he said, using the nickname he had given her, "always try to find the good things about your friends."

When Jeanna returned from her job as assistant manager of a convenience store in Colville, she and Tom chatted for a while about the day. He said good night to his daughters and then went to get his own good night's sleep before his first run in the truck the next day. On his way to bed he stopped off in the bathroom. After a while, Jeanna gasped, suddenly realizing that she had heard the water running far too long in the bathroom sink.

She and Lori pounded on the door. No response. Louder knocks and desperate shouts brought still no response, so Jeanna battered the door with her shoulder until it yielded. They found Tom lying on the floor, his weakened heart no longer beating.

At Tom's funeral, Pastor Hindrik Van Dyjken assured the mourners who packed the sanctuary and spilled over into the basement that Thomas Le Roy Kennedy was in the presence of his Lord. "His new walk was prompted," he said, "by the book *Left Behind*." He told how Tom, after reading the novel, "became a shepherd to his family. He phoned his friends, he talked to me at length—he became the fictional Rayford Steele in the flesh."

Tom's ashes rest beside a twenty-two-acre lake near the ranch house, in a rustic crypt ringed by a rail fence and marked by a twinkling lantern. To his family and friends left behind, Tom joins with the fictional pastor Vernon Billings, who is seen on a videotape in the novel, calling forth, in words true and plain:

"'Death is swallowed up in victory. O Death, where is your sting? O Hades, where is your victory?' The sting of death is sin, and the strength of sin is the law. But thanks be to God, who gives us the victory through our Lord Jesus Christ."

"Are these books written simply for entertainment? Or are you trying to bring people to accept God in their lives? If the latter is true, then I think Dr. LaHaye can help me by answering my questions about God. I'm a scientist doing what religious people are adamantly opposed to (in Kansas, anyway). So, I've been ignoring organized religion."

—BROOKE T.

"I gave my life to Christ after reading the first book. See you at the Rapture!"

—BROTHER LEONARD

"Not until I started reading your books did I really understand what it is to be a Christian. I'm stoked to learn more about God and the Bible."

—BRAD H., U.S. ARMY

"I'm not 'officially' a Christian. Never thought I needed to be saved. But these books are the best, most exciting spiritual books I've ever read. Now I will *not* be 'left behind.' I'm speechless. Could that have been your plan all along?"

—BOB P.

WITH HIS
DYING BREATH

SOME THROUGH GREAT TRIALS,

BUT GOD GIVES A SONG.

—FROM THE HYMN, "GOD LEADS US ALONG,"

BY G.A. YOUNG

In the first month of his first pastorate, John Petrilli had his hands full making sure that the electrical power and phone lines were functioning in his new church in Geneseo, Illinois, along the Mississippi River. When he casually mentioned to his board chairman that he needed a barber, he said, "See Bill. I've gone to him for years."

The following morning, Pastor John walked into Bill's shop and asked, "You know how to do a layer cut?"

Bill snickered. "Hop into the chair."

Holding a mirror afterward, the pastor exclaimed, "Amazing! That's the best haircut I've ever had! I must apologize to you, sir."

"Well," Bill said shyly, "no harm done. I was trained by the best, back on the East Coast. Had my first position on Fifth Avenue in New York City."

Thus began what became a lifelong friendship.

One month later, on a sunny Friday afternoon, Pastor John was interrupted in his study by an unexpected phone call from his board chairman. "Bad news about Bill," he began. "He's been diagnosed with inoperable cancer of the liver."

John thanked the chairman and quickly dialed Bill's home, where the barber confirmed the bad news. "Yep, it's nailed me," he said. "Gotta go out of town for treatments beginning next Monday. Say, Pastor, I need someone to chauffeur me. You wouldn't be—?"

"Too busy? Bill, I'd be happy to drive you to your doctor."

On the fifty-mile round-trip, the men swapped stories about growing up, about siblings and parents and disappointments. The barber told how he had come west to settle in the small Midwest town to escape all sorts of problems. He'd been married several times, and most things he'd tried had just sort of turned around and walloped him. Bill seemed to be packing into his conversation with the pastor everything he'd wanted to confess but had been too busy to get around to.

John visited Bill every day at his home, to the delight of the barber. During one visit, Bill's nurse told John that she needed someone to stay with Bill until ten o'clock the following evening. He immediately volunteered, but before he took up his post, he phoned as many in his congregation as he could to request prayer for the dying barber who needed the Savior.

The following night, John asked Bill if he wanted company. Bill declined, so John settled into a rocker outside his room and continued reading the novel *Left Behind*. As he read about the Rapture snatching passengers off Rayford Steele's 747 bound for London, God strongly tugged at his heart about the urgency of Bill's situation. With only fifteen minutes left on his shift, he became determined to try once more.

With an urgent prayer in his heart, John cracked open the door to Bill's bedroom. "May I come in?"

Bill nodded weakly.

As John spoke, he sensed the Holy Spirit using the bridge of friendship God had built to allow him access to Bill's needy spirit.

"Bill, we haven't known each other very long, but there's something very important I have to share with you," the pastor began. "Jesus Christ died as our substitute so that we don't have to suffer for our sins. Put your trust in Him, Bill," he said, "and that failing body full of pain will be gloriously replaced with a new body that will never again suffer pain or death."

As the clock in the living room struck ten, Bill

prayed the prayer of a repentant sinner. That night he was born into the kingdom of God, and inherited eternal life. "Thank you, Pastor," he whispered.

The next day, John was driving by Bill's house when he felt an irresistible urge to stop and see him. The nurse met him anxiously at the door, explaining that Bill was breathing his last. John hurried to his friend's bedside. Bill could no longer speak.

"I had never seen anyone die," John said later, "but I acted on impulse and gently held his hand. After about fifteen minutes, Bill let out a deep sigh and stopped breathing. He regained his breath moments later, but after a few more seconds, he breathed his last and passed into eternity."

To comfort Bill's weeping nurse, John softly assured her that Bill was now in a better place where there is no pain. Three days later, he addressed Bill's friends at his funeral service. He read Psalm 23, Bill's favorite. Their friend had passed safely through the "valley of the shadow of death" by placing his faith in Jesus Christ as his Savior and Lord.

Pastor Petrilli keeps that copy of *Left Behind* close by his reading chair, where it reminds him constantly of the wonderful privilege he had in leading a successful but lonely man to the Lord.

"I'm the midday personality at a radio station in this Colorado town, a student of religion for a long time—more prone to Buddhist teachings, though I've read the Koran and the Bible. I was raised Methodist, but never was religious. Since moving here I've seen *Left Behind* in homes of new friends, as well as in bookstores. Finally read it and *Tribulation Force*. The books made me ask tough questions of myself. I believe I'll be ready to commit to a church soon. Thanks for giving me a way to fill in the spiritual void I've been mired in for some time."

—TOMMIE

"I was truly an amazing sight to my wife and children, sitting there in my easy chair reading the books with a King James Bible and the NIV opened to Revelation. Being a pilot, I identify with Rayford, but I especially enjoyed the accounts of the witnesses at the Wailing Wall. If you ever need technical advice related to aviation, I would be pleased to help."

—CAPTAIN DAVE, ALPHAJET INT'L.

"I am going to church this Sunday to be a devout worshiper. Funny, sort of what Buck did. 'Course, I didn't have the Russian Air Force falling all around me. I find myself thirsty, very thirsty, for the Word. Can't get enough."

—JASON B.

THE BORROWED BOOK

HIS TRUTH ENDURES TO

ALL GENERATIONS.

—PSALM 100:5, NKJV

Jimmie Duane Fulkerson, Jr., awoke early one Sunday morning in Roswell, New Mexico. As Kathy, his wife, slept soundly, he slipped out of bed, put on his slippers, and soon had coffee percolating merrily in the kitchen.

As he poured two cups, Jimmie noticed a book on the kitchen table. He carried the coffee into the bedroom, kissed his wife awake, as was his habit, then asked, "Where'd you get the book?"

"You mean *Left Behind*?" Kathy asked, sitting up

and propping a pillow behind her. "Oh, I borrowed it from a neighbor."

"Mind if I look at it?" Jimmie asked.

"No, go ahead," his wife said, surprised by her husband's sudden interest in reading. The wiry lumberman, standing six feet two inches tall, had always been an outdoor type, not a lover of books. But he settled into his favorite recliner and began to read.

To Kathy's amazement, her husband was still reading at lunchtime . . . into the afternoon . . . and all evening. Finally he snapped the book shut and stood up. "Can't wait to read *Tribulation Force*," he said.

Laying the book on the coffee table, he turned to his wife with a curious question: "If I were to get religious, would you still love me?" While she was looking at him in disbelief, he hit her with another astonishing statement: "Let's go to church as a family this coming Sunday."

Jimmie continued to talk about God, about Christianity, about dying, about salvation, and about the end of the age. To Kathy's chagrin, Jimmie even outlined for her the method he desired for his burial—cremation and a celebration.

Between the arrival of each book in the Left Behind series Jimmie read his Bible. Sometimes he read it on his lunch break at work, sitting on a pile of lumber at Dodson's Wholesale Lumber Company. Sometimes he read in his truck parked at the high school football stadium across from the lumberyard, and sometimes he read at home in front of his son, JayDe. Although Kathy had made sure, through the years, that their sons became members of St. Andrews Episcopal Church and were baptized and confirmed, they seldom made it to worship services and rarely, if ever, as a complete family. Jimmie was never comfortable at church, but because nothing was more important to him than his wife and sons, he did go from time to time.

When Jimmie began reading the Left Behind books and casting aside old habits, his elder son, Brandon, was in his second year of college, and he had been recruited to pitch for a New York Yankees' AAA team. His younger son, JayDe, a high school freshman, was active in a youth group at Christ's Church.

"What's it like at that church?" his father asked. "I'd like to take a look."

To his surprise, Jimmie loved the service. The pastor's messages explained and elaborated on the issues raised in *Left Behind* and the other novels. Then, in the spring of 2000, Jimmie attended a Walk to Emmaus seminar sponsored by his sister, Donna Todd, in Sacramento, New Mexico. While on this walk, a seventy-two-hour simulated journey with Christ based on the biblical walk by the Savior to the town of Emmaus, Jimmie knelt and prayed at the foot of a cross situated at a scenic site in a nearby campground named the Point of Silence.

On that trip, Jimmie gave his heart to the Savior, even professing before an audience. Then JayDe surprised his parents that spring on Mother's Day by rededicating his life publicly to Christ; he was baptized following this confession of faith.

"It's the most awesome gift for a child to give," Jimmie remarked.

Meanwhile, in Tampa, Florida, Brandon had become associated with a morally strong Christian buddy named Clay and had started to attend Bible study classes. Shortly after hearing his father's big news, he phoned his parents with good news of his own: "The most exciting thing in my entire life just happened to me. I gave my life to Christ." The circle grew tighter as each son became committed to the same goals, determined to make their lives a reflection of Christ's love to everyone they met. At forty-three, Jimmie was enjoying a wonderfully sweet life. His job was secure, and his family united. Others who knew Jimmie wished they could be as strong, fulfilled, and happy.

On the evening of November 1, 2000, Jimmie went to the kitchen to scoop his nightly dish of ice cream while Kathy took a shower. When she later found him in the kitchen, he was making a mess and dripping ice cream. He hadn't even eaten any of it. "I've got a bad headache," he said, pushing aside his dessert. A few moments later, he collapsed onto the couch. Medics from the Roswell Fire Department could not resuscitate him, so he was flown to Covenant Hospital in Lubbock, Texas, where they quickly determined that he needed brain surgery—what turned out to be a ten-hour procedure—if they were to save his life.

Brandon flew home from Tampa to be with his mother and to lend support to his brother. In that sad circle of tears, Kathy, her two sons, Grandma Jo, sisters Sandra, Donna, and Shona, and brother Lindell, stood around Jimmie's bed and prayed as medics unhooked the wires, tubes, cables, and electronic devices that had failed to restore Jimmy's life. Finding the peace that only Jesus gives, the Fulkersons gave back to God their husband, father, brother, and son. One of them had brought a little CD player, and the chorus, "We will dance on the streets that are golden . . . " filled their hearts with hope and joy.

They could rejoice because Jimmie had read and believed the testimony of Pastor Vernon Billings, pastor of the fictional New Hope Village Church featured in *Left Behind*, who recited the Bible passage found in the fifteenth chapter of 1 Corinthians, written by the apostle Paul:

> *Behold, I tell you a mystery: We shall not all sleep, but we shall all be changed—in a moment, in the twinkling of an eye, at the last trumpet. For the trumpet will sound, and the dead will be raised incorruptible, and we shall be changed. For this corruptible must put on incorruption, and this mortal must put on immortality.*

The weather turned unseasonably cold the day of Jimmie's memorial service, and then a blizzard blew in from the north. Roads into Roswell were clogged with

snow. The high school dismissed classes. More than
five hundred people gathered to pay their respects and
to remember the gentle man whom so many had come
to love. JayDe played his guitar and Donna sang
Jimmie's favorite song, "On Eagle's Wings."

> Come, breathe in me . . .
> And I will rise on eagle's wings.

When the storm cut off electrical power, flickering
candles struggled to banish the darkness as Brandon
thanked everyone for their prayers and loving support.
He then read a tribute to his father he had composed,
titled "Memories of You." It ended:

> I remember a man so proud, so strong, so noble,
> so sensitive and caring,
> And that man is my dad, Jimmie Duane
> Fulkerson.

Brandon later married Kelli Lynn Campbell, a beautiful
girl he met at the hospital the night of his father's
death. To Kathy, she was "an angel sent to comfort us
when Jimmie left us."

As each new Left Behind novel is published, Kathy
reads it, adds it to her bookshelf, and eagerly awaits the
next one. As Jimmie did, many are finding the path to
God, a source of understanding about redemption, and
the hope of seeing loved ones again.

The Mayor of Roswell declared April 7, 2001 Jimmie Fulkerson Day. On that date, the Noon Optimist Little League kicked off an entire year of celebration for Jimmie and his family, "because of all the time they have invested in the league."

Kathy continues in her role as coordinator for Teen CBS (Christian Bible Study). She is active in her church, plans to travel abroad with JayDe on mission trips, and still praises God for the years she had with her handsome Jimmie. And she is glad that she placed the borrowed book, *Left Behind,* on the coffee table one morning in 1999, that Jimmie spotted it, that he took time to read it, and that he is in heaven today because of it.

"I'm glad I let my husband read it first," she says with a smile.

"I was born into a family of Christians but I never understood the message of salvation. God helped me see the truth. Who knows where I'd be now if it hadn't been for those books!"

—DEVVORA P.

"At a baptismal service last night in our church, three out of ten candidates were *Left Behind* converts. One, a real character, said he saw the title *Assassins* and thought it was 'pretty cool for a Christian book.' Evidently enormous changes occurred in that man's life. Got him thinking. He came to Calvary and was saved. I thought of you guys when they mentioned the books."

—DIANE D.

"I wasn't halfway into *Left Behind* when I reached for my Bible. I cried . . . had goose bumps, and experienced a chill in my back."

—THERESA K.

"Last summer, I started reading the Left Behind books, but my friend was totally not interested. I took all the books I had and told her to read them at her leisure. A couple of months later, she was out buying the collection for herself. She started going to church and learning about God. Just two weeks before she was killed, she dedicated her heart and life to God. I want to thank you for those books."

—DONYA A.

DEATH CAME EARLY

HE BEING DEAD STILL SPEAKS.

—HEBREWS 11:4, NKJV

At 10 A.M. on Wednesday, April 25, 2001, David Lee Goff prepared to die in Huntsville, Texas, for the 1990 murder of Michael McGuire. Condemned by an unbelieving jury, appeals courts, and untruthful witnesses, David had given up all hope of being exonerated. Something bigger than all the lies and hopelessness had taken hold of him, though, so he carefully scrawled on a piece of paper: "I am being wronged . . . "

David paused, leaned back in his metal chair, and let his mind drift back to the heat and humidity of a late summer day in 1969. As usual, there'd been nothing to do. David, only fifteen then, had joined with a group of older boys to run the streets and have some fun. One had a loaded pistol. They used it to steal money from a convenience store, and killed two people who tried to stop them. When the police arrived, one of the older boys poked David in the chest and said, "Look, kid, you take the rap for this one, get it? A few years in juvenile detention and you're out! *We'd* get life in prison."

David took the blame and served out his teen years looking at the concrete floors, walls, and ceilings of Ferguson Prison Unit at Midway, Texas, before returning home to Ft. Worth.

Finally free at twenty, David entered life "outside" with a passion. He immediately got a job and worked tirelessly in the catering department of a top Ft. Worth hotel, where he became a supervisor. He also started his college education and was doing well. Then one day he heard the police were looking for him, so he went to the police station to see what they wanted. He was arrested and indicted on capital murder charges.

With David's prison record, it was easy for the prosecutor to get a conviction—especially after David's witnesses were not allowed to testify. Out of the nine names he had given his attorney, the investigator only called three. Asked if they would testify for him, they all said yes but were never given a chance. While they waited to testify, they heard that David had been convicted and sentenced to death.

At the Ellis Unit in Huntsville, David wrote poetry and several book-length manuscripts, and he read relentlessly. No family or friends remembered him with a visit or even a phone call. For seven years he received no personal letters. Finally, during the last couple of years before his scheduled execution, David developed some pen pals in Belgium, but only Chaplain Jack, a minister who visited the prison regularly, ever befriended him.

As nine and a half years passed on Death Row, David not only *doubted* God, he *blamed* him for the fact that he was receiving punishment for a crime he hadn't committed. Frustration, hate, despair, and hopelessness consumed his thoughts. One day he found a copy of *Left Behind* in the prison library and he began to read it. It was then that "the renewal of my mind and my faith began. The one message that screamed at me was that only God is faithful. *Only God?* I asked myself. Yes, I could buy that. Every book in the series has changed me. Hate went out of my heart. Through my trials, the Lord has sustained me."

In his prison cell one day, David wrote a letter to Tim LaHaye, a personal friend of Chaplain Jack. He laid out his situation, then asked a favor:

> The pace of capital appeals has moved my case along with little anticipation that I will be alive much beyond August of this year.
>
> *Assassins* is due in August. I would very much

like to be able to read at least one more part of the story before I die. My inquiry is whether it is possible to arrange to purchase a copy of *Assassins* in advance of the actual date of availability. Irene Wilcox, a friend of yours who works with her husband, Jack, in a prison ministry here, thought you might be able to send me the new book before I die.

If there is any way that you could help me, I would be grateful. I look forward to reading more of the vivid vision of God's faithfulness toward those who are totally faithful to him. I, for one, would like to say thank you to both you and Mr. Jenkins, if nothing else. I am very grateful to the both of you for stirring the spirit within me.

I will await word from you with patience.

In His Peace,

David L. Goff

Both Tim LaHaye and Jerry Jenkins signed a copy of the manuscript, and the publisher sent it to David Lee Goff. On April 25, 2001, he was transferred from the Allen B. Polunsky Unit to the Huntsville (Walls) Unit for execution. There he wrote on a piece of paper: "Let all debt be canceled, whether real or imagined." He submitted his body to the executioners and died, later to be laid to rest at a cemetery in Arlington, Texas. Though unfulfilled on this earth, he was prepared to enter into his eternal rest with Christ as his Lord and Savior. Chaplain Jack notified the authors of the Left Behind series and related David's story to others. His poems were never published, but David's name is written down in the best place of all—in the Lamb's Book of Life for eternity.

"Some tragic happenings made me mad at God. I questioned my faith and Christianity. *Left Behind* touched me, because I'd never got the picture of the Second Coming—children missing, great crashes . . . It became clear that if God came back, my small son would go to be with him, no matter what. I wasn't sure I would, too. I have since rededicated my life to the Lord and sorted out my feelings toward the sudden deaths of my baby brother, my cousin, and my aunt. I am hurting but I now have a whole new reason to live—for God!"

—LEE H.

"I was raised in Judaism, but my wife and children are making me aware of Christianity. The words of Ben-Judah have made me wonder about my salvation because his studies led him to conclude that Jesus is the Messiah. I would be interested in a book dedicated to Dr. Ben Judah's research."

—JACOB S.

"The relative of an employee of Focus on the Family became a believer after reading the Left Behind series. A fatal illness gave him no hope of living until October 30, 2001, but he desperately wanted to read *Desecration* before he died. His wife went to the Family Book Store to beg for a copy. They said no one had any because they would not be released early. So the wife prayed, 'Lord, this is all my husband wants before he

dies. Either provide one or give me peace about it.'
The next day, Jerry Jenkins sent the man a copy, fulfilling the man's dying wish."

—AUTHOR UNKNOWN

A PRISON
EPISTLE

HOW ELSE BUT THROUGH

A BROKEN HEART

MAY LORD CHRIST ENTER IN?

—OSCAR WILDE

Although Eddie found himself incarcerated at
length inside the Florida penal system, he didn't just
while away the days.

In 1997, he earned a bachelor of science degree in
business administration by mail from Hamilton
University, followed by a masters in business administration in October 1998. In 1999, he earned an accredited asset management specialist degree from the
College for Financial Planning, and also designation

as a chartered mutual fund counselor. To top off his prison education, Eddie completed a course in writing for children, offered by the Institute of Children's Literature. These accomplishments were a spectacular achievement for a man behind bars, but was Eddie satisfied?

"I felt as though I had done *nothing*," he wrote. "I even wrote two novel-length manuscripts, but as soon as I mailed them I knew that wasn't it either."

Discouraged, he languished in prison for a year and a half until a friend asked him to read *Left Behind*. When he came to the scene where Rayford Steele, the tough airline captain, bows his head by the side of his bed and weeps, Eddie gave his own life to Christ. That was on a Wednesday. On Sunday, he affirmed his vows as a newborn Christian in the prison's nondenominational chapel.

"I now know what was missing—Jesus Christ, my Lord and Savior," Eddie said. "I don't know if I'll ever be a published author, whether I'll ply my trade as a financial advisor and planner, or whether I'll become an accredited asset management specialist, but I do know one thing for certain: God has forgiven my sins, and He will take me to heaven.

"I am surrounded by guys [in prison] who think they're macho and tough," Eddie said. "I have news for them. A truly tough, innocent man was crucified for all of us. Think about it! Spikes through His ankles and wrists, excruciating pain, having to push His weight up on those spikes just to utter a sentence or two—*that* is true toughness and bravery. And you know what? He didn't *have* to do it. He could have left us all to suffer for our sins.

"We could all be left behind. That's the message I plan to take to as many prisons and youth facilities as I can when I get out of here someday. Because I discovered *Him* here," he said, "He won't leave me behind."

"After our pastor invited anyone with good news to share it, a guy stood up and said that for thirty years he'd been praying for a college buddy who was a wild character. He said, 'I shared the gospel with this dude numerous times with no effect.'

"Then his college friend phoned to say that he had read in only two days a book titled *Left Behind*. As a result, he became a Christian. He asked the guy from our church, 'Why didn't you ever tell me about this stuff?'

"Our church member said, 'I've been telling you this stuff for ten years.'

"'Not like *that!*' his friend said."

—LARRY S.

"God has shown me clearly through these books that what we believe should truly effect *every* aspect of how we live."

—AMY S.

"At the beginning of this school year, I couldn't seem to get out of being depressed about little stuff. Then I started reading *Apollyon* at school. My world history teacher came over and asked about the book. I was kinda shocked, but several days later he showed me he had the whole series. In a high school overrun with Wicca and atheism, I get a lot of laughs when I bring my Bible to school. I just wish Jesus would come soon."

—JESS C.

THE HEALING PLACE

FOR MY DAYS DISAPPEAR

LIKE SMOKE.

—PSALM 102:3

Shane and a buddy found benches near a downtown Louisville motel and lit their glass pipe to smoke some crystal meth. "How much did this cost you?" his friend asked, shaking the bag.

Shane thought a moment then answered, "Everything."

"*Every*thing?"

"Every last thing I had on earth. I got thrown out of my father's house because of that little bag of speed. He took his car away from me, and now I have no way to get to work. That means no job."

As Shane and his partner used up the rest of the drug, he thought of other friends—addicts, mostly: A dancer, a transvestite, a lawyer, a clerk from city hall, a cab driver, a kid in his teens—people from every walk of life. As the sun set in the western sky, Shane and his fellow addict sat in silence, their thoughts accusing them as their moods darkened.. Shane was twenty-eight, and this wasn't how he thought things would end up. If they'd even thought of God, they would have said He was far away and uninvolved—that is, if He even existed.

The money required to sustain Shane's habit came from many sources. Until he moved in with his father, his mother paid his bills. Whatever he earned at a job went to purchase more drugs—crystal meth, heroin, marijuana. When his mother refused to give him any more money, he pawned every stick of furniture. Then he pawned his car and lost it. His parents replaced his car twice before throwing up their hands in exasperation and saying, "No more!"

Then, on August 8, 2000, one of Shane's best friends, Aaron, died from a drug overdose. The tragedy seemed to energize Shane and fill him with a resolve to quit. He really meant it this time. But he struggled on for nine more agonizing months before he found the strength to ask for help.. On May 9, 2001, he checked out of his hotel, took a bus downtown to Market Street, and rang the doorbell at the Morgan Center to check in to their rehabilitation program.

The staff at Morgan gave Shane hope that he might

be able to recover. He wanted to do it not only for himself but also for Aaron, to bring an end to ten devastating, empty years of drug abuse.

Shane's first visitors were his folks. His stepmother came in carrying two books. One was a Bible, and the other was a copy of *Left Behind*. His father watched suspiciously to see if this trip to rehab was just another gimmick, or if his son was finally serious about straightening out his life.

When Shane first arrived at the Morgan Center, there were forty-five men, ranging in age from seventeen to sixty-five, in the program. Eventually, 110 addicts had been squeezed into the same space. A minister named Otis became Shane's mentor.

Otis explained the Scriptures to his new friend, and told him often about the end times as presented in *Left Behind*. Otis firmly believed in the prophecies from both the Old and New Testaments of the Bible. For the first time in his life, Shane had a true mentor.

In recovery, the patients were urged to get their own personal history down in writing, so Shane poured his sad story into spiral notebooks. He had been hooked on crystal meth for five years, then switched to heroin, which kept him hooked and high for nearly another five years. His horror stories could match just about anyone's at the clinic. The real drama lay not so much in *taking* the drugs as in what the addicts would do to *buy* them. Several were former dealers who themselves had gotten hooked, and many formerly respectable citizens were there, thus proving that addiction is no respecter of persons. Everybody had seen someone die of an overdose or get shot.

As Shane progressed with his recovery, he and his father drew close again. His father knew that Shane had to do the work himself, but he offered guidance from his experience of working through the steps of Alcoholics Anonymous, which he had learned a decade earlier in breaking the grip of alcoholism. He advised Shane to live "one day at a time."

The first thing Shane did on the outside was to attend Beulah Land Baptist Church, where his uncle Doug was pastor. There Doug was, standing in the pulpit preaching from—of all books—the book of Revelation, the very book Shane had been studying at the rehab center.

"Uncle Doug's message touched my heart so dramatically that I knew God was calling me forward," Shane said. "I was both scared and excited. I longed to be forgiven of my sins that day. I longed to forget the years I had wasted, to feel God's love through my Lord, to have the warmth of my family's love again—love that I had ignored for so long."

As Shane stood at the front of the church, Pastor Doug invited members to gather around and express their love for a sinner who had come home. A line of eager faces formed and arms reached out to embrace Shane and to welcome him into the fellowship of believers.

Two weeks later, Shane stood up again, this time

on the steps of the baptistry to give his testimony on the day of his baptism. His mother hugged him and whispered, "I'm *proud* of you."

"I could see that pride shining in her eyes," Shane said. "That was a special gift from God that I'll always remember. And when I was submerged and then came up out of the water, I felt relieved of wasted years, cleansed from unholy living. I understood what the pastor meant when he said a new life in Christ awaited me. I was ready to begin doing what He called me to do."

Each day now, Shane eagerly dons his uniform, installs his microphone, and prepares to meet customers at an Arby's drive-through restaurant across the Ohio River from Louisville.

"You'd be surprised how many times I have a chance to talk about Jesus," he said. "People from all walks of life who come there to eat, and my coworkers as well, want to talk about God and the Left Behind books. Instead of being a pilot or a famous newspaper reporter like in *Left Behind*, I'm a fast-food employee who has the same responsibility as the Tribulation Force to spread God's word. That's my mission, and I'll continue until the day Jesus comes to take me home."

In a letter to a friend, Shane wrote:

> Drugs—you destroyer of life.
> Drugs—you almost destroyed mine.
> Drugs—but His love for me was stronger.
> Drugs—no high of yours can compare with God's.

"I wandered away from God for most of my young life. I didn't stop believing; I just didn't give him my life.

"My father's only request from God was for me to find Him again. His prayer was answered, but not in the way he would've wanted. My life was turned upside down after Dad first started praying.

"I phoned him one night in tears. He could barely understand what I was babbling. 'If God has a reason for everything that happens to us,' I asked, 'then please explain why He put me through *this*.'

"Dad and I talked for a long time that night. He told me to ask God to forgive me, and ask Him to come into my heart.

"That night I lay on my bed and prayed as I've never prayed before. When I did what Dad told me to do, the most amazing feeling came over me. I knew God had taken all my worries into His hands. My heart felt lighter. I felt a peace I haven't felt in years. I knew right then that I could allow God to handle things for me in His own way and time.

"Dad sent me the *Left Behind* series. I felt a connection to the ones left behind. It was me *right there in that book!* I pray now that I'll be taken, too, with Dad."

—DAWN G.

PART FOUR

GIVING GOD THE GLORY

A brilliant light from heaven suddenly beamed down upon him!

He fell to the ground and heard a voice saying to him,

"Saul! Saul! Why are you persecuting me?"

Acts 9:3-4

TWENTY YEARS
IN THE
WAITING ROOM

―――――――――――――――――――――――

THE LORD'S SERVANTS MUST

. . . BE KIND TO EVERYONE . . .

ABLE TO TEACH EFFECTIVELY

AND BE PATIENT WITH

DIFFICULT PEOPLE. . . .

PERHAPS GOD WILL CHANGE

THOSE PEOPLE'S HEARTS,

AND THEY WILL BELIEVE

THE TRUTH.

―2 TIMOTHY 2:24-25

Christina Lapiska, a nurse-in-training at Bob
Jones University, stood at the chapel microphone on a
Day of Prayer in the spring of 2002, and told a fascinat-
ing story of God's patience in bringing to salvation her
beloved grandparents, "Tut" (William) and "Mommom"
(Peggy) Lapiska.

"My grandparents never considered themselves to be
religious," Christine told her schoolmates in Greenville,
South Carolina, "but always thought of themselves as
good, moral people. Because of this, they could not
understand their need for salvation because they could
not admit they were sinners."

Christina's father, Brad, and his family had
witnessed to his parents since Christina was a little
girl. However, her grandparents steadfastly refused to
listen and made it clear that they did not want to hear
about Jesus Christ being a Savior.

"All my life, the rest of my family and I have been
praying that the Lord would soften their hearts and
save their souls," she said.

In the summer of 1972, Brad had received the Lord
as his Savior through an evangelical youth group that
he and his cousins attended. His father and mother
shrugged and decided that their son's fling with evangelical Christianity couldn't hurt him. The Lapiska
family then moved to Colorado, and Brad attended
Colorado State University.

After graduating from CSU in 1977, Brad married
Patricia Goslee and joined the United States Marine

Corps. They had two daughters, Julie and Christina. In 1987, God called Brad to preach, so he resigned his commission and left for Greenville, South Carolina to attend Bob Jones University for his seminary training.

"My grandparents could not understand why Dad would leave a promising career in the Marine Corps, move his family to an unknown area, and go back to school—all for 'a religion,'" Christina continued.

The senior Lapiskas lived only four hours away in Tennessee, allowing for frequent visits. During each visit, Tut and Mommom would observe, and occasionally sit in on, family devotions and prayer time. But they steadfastly refused to discuss salvation.

In 1994, Brad became senior pastor of Engleside Baptist Church in Virginia. Six years later, a special worship service on Veteran's Day would honor the brave men and women who had fought to keep America free. Tut was a veteran of the Korean War and, like his son, patriotic to the core. Brad invited his father to participate in the Veteran's Day service.

"To our surprise," Christina told her audience, "he agreed. I immediately began praying more than ever for Mommom and Tut's salvation. I asked my prayer group and classes to pray as well."

Following the service, Brad invited everyone in his audience to make certain they had confessed their sins and received the pardon that Jesus Christ, the Son of God, willingly offered. At the end of that prayer, Tut raised his hand.

"I don't know why it's taken me so long to realize my need," he said as he and Brad embraced, tears streaming down their faces.

Patricia immediately phoned her daughters at college. Christina blanketed the campus with news of her grandpa's conversion, which she "couldn't believe had finally taken place after twenty years. The Lord answered our prayers," she said. Still, Mommom tenaciously declined to pray the sinner's prayer.

For Christmas that year, Christina gave Mommom and Tut a copy of *Left Behind*. When Tut was finished reading it, Mommom began. "Much of what I'd been telling her was in the pages of that book," Christina said. "I knew its message would hit home."

It did! Mommom sped past Tut and outpaced even Christina and her mother in reading *all* the Left Behind novels. She began asking her son questions not only about matters of doctrine and the Bible but why Tut had changed so much, and "What does it really mean to be a Christian?"

And then it happened. At Engleside Baptist Church's 2001 Veteran's Day Service, exactly one year to the day after Tut became a believer, Mommom bowed her head, acknowledged her sin, and said yes to the Savior.

"My son is fourteen and has been reluctant to study and learn about Christ. He loves science fiction and fantasy novels. His best friend told him how great the Left Behind novels are. Now Mical is reading the series, looking up Bible references, and talking to his church youth group about what they say. He no longer argues about attending Sunday school and pays close attention in church instead of daydreaming or falling asleep. He told me I should read one, so I said, "Okay, *one*," just to please him and keep the connection. Surprise! God showed me I've been neglectful in my faith. I've returned after just "marking time." I'm reading my Bible again and praising the Lord."

—TED S.

"My friend wouldn't hear of going to a fundamental church, much less read the Bible. She was persuaded to read *Left Behind,* and then phoned when she got to *Nicolae* and asked me to pray for her. Later, she accepted the Lord as her Savior and is now reading God's Holy Book, the Bible."

—CONNIE S.

IT'S NEVER
TOO LATE

HE PLANTS TREES TO

BENEFIT ANOTHER

GENERATION.

—CAECILIUS STATIUS

The co-owner of an auto repair shop in Kennesaw, Georgia, pulled Pastor Ike aside one Sunday morning at Northstar Church and asked for help.

"It's my parents," he began. "I'm just not sure they know what it means to be born again. I am so new in my faith that I feel uncomfortable discussing it with people I respect so much—like my parents. I would like someone who's been a believer for a long time to talk to them."

Ike suggested getting together with the young man's parents at a local restaurant to have a chat about Christ.

A few days later, Ike set up the appointment to meet with the parents and talk to them face-to-face. After the initial introductions, and before Ike had a chance to share his faith, the mother blurted out, "Could you please tell us how to be saved?" Ike was happy to oblige.

The couple explained how, along with some friends, they had read a series of books called Left Behind. Ike, familiar with the novels, realized that the printed word had planted the seed, God's spirit had watered the crop, and now he would have the privilege of harvesting the fruit.

Pastor Ike reached for their hands across the table and explained clearly the simple message of hope in Christ the Lord. Then he led them in a prayer of commitment. It was like dessert before the meal.

Two weeks later, the new Christians invited Ike to come to the lake resort north of Atlanta, where they lived, and meet several neighbors who also had an interest in being born again. They also had been reading the novels, and Ike once again found himself harvesting where others had sown.

Seven couples that evening, surrounded by the elegant furnishings of a beautiful home, bowed their heads and repeated the sinner's prayer together. Not everyone in the group was saved that night, but several made it clear that this was their first experience in having a personal experience with Jesus Christ.

"The Left Behind books are wonderful ice-breakers," Ike said. "It used to be if I were traveling on a plane and I said I was a pastor, the person inquiring about my occupation would look around for another seat. Now, many lean close and say something like, "You know, I've been wondering about these—these books. Do you really believe, as a minister, that they are accurate?"

"The Left Behind books?"

"Yes! Those are the ones. Tell me about all this Armageddon stuff."

Ike calls the series "the air force of Christian evangelistic strategy. It softens up the ground by dropping 'bombs' of truth, thus allowing 'foot soldiers' to share their faith with willing hearts already open to the gospel."

Knowing that their days are numbered, elderly citizens all over the world are eager to kneel at the Cross for deliverance from the penalty of sin and enjoy a future with God in heaven—beyond the clutches of the Antichrist, outside the plagues of demon locusts, ferocious horsemen, and trumpet judgments that will occur during the coming tribulation.

"It's never too late," Pastor Ike says.

"I now know I have to get my life in order, starting with Jesus as my Savior and Lord."

—J. F. HARPER

"These books have caused me to do some serious thinking about the end times. I'm preparing. After all, Jesus might come back tomorrow!"

—JOSH H.

"I'm here at Ball State in Muncie, Indiana, and I'm reading your novel. I feel very, very different now. I'm giving my life to Christ. By the way, I'm happy!"

—TODD J.

"My friend Dale interprets for the deaf at a local college. One of the women she helps is Stephanie, who has severe cerebral palsy. Dale found out she's a Christian, so she gave her *Left Behind*. Stephanie in turn gave it to her boyfriend, Chip, and then to her regular caregiver. Both have become Christians and *all three* now attend church with Dale!"

—GRACE N.

AN AWAKENING AT FIRST CHURCH

HOLD FAITHFULNESS AND

SINCERITY AS FIRST

PRINCIPLES.

—CONFUCIUS

For the life of him, Charles Robert "Bob" Davis of Eureka, California, couldn't remember meeting Tim LaHaye and Jerry Jenkins, yet those authors had his life down cold in a story titled *Left Behind.*

Bob said, "Reverend Bruce at the altar, crying out to God about how he had all the right answers, talked the right talk, looked the part of a true follower of Christ but deep down was 'on his own'—that was *me!*"

Bob's church didn't really have a Christian perspective. When the pastor spoke, he would review books, tell stories, and make insightful or clever comments about the passing sociopolitical scene. He avoided altar calls and sermons that might offend, winked at sin, tolerated just about any humanistic doctrine, and never gave his congregation the impression that any of it was all that important, much less a matter of eternal life or death. The Bible was never acknowledged as the inspired, inerrant Word of God. It made the pastor uncomfortable to presume to preach the gospel as good news. Nor would he recommend to his congregation that they read and believe the Bible, pray, tell others about salvation, or live holy lives before God.

In a Sunday school class one morning, a fifty-year member suggested that there should be a third gate between the broad road to destruction and the narrow road to salvation. In his words, it was "just not fair" to have only a wide gate and a narrow gate. The notion was roundly affirmed. Bob and Judy Davis sat numbly through nearly a decade of this apostasy. Like the fictional Rayford Steele in the Left Behind novels, the Davises looked at the church as a cozy social club that had no business telling people how they should live their lives. Then Monty and Diana Holsapple, a couple "very much in love with Jesus," came into their lives. They gave Bob and Judy a copy of the novel *Left Behind* and urged them to read it.

What effect did it have on their lives? "Does the phrase 'night and day' cover it?" Bob quipped, a wide

smile on his face. For more than a decade, he had
served as an elder without a purpose in the church.
"I taught a few adult Sunday school classes, was
respected by most people, and looked like a real
Christian, but deep down inside I knew I was a fake."

Inspired by biblical truths he discovered in *Left
Behind*, Bob began to ruffle feathers at First Church.
The pastor held views quite opposed to the story line
in the novel. For example, he claimed that Moses
didn't write the first five books of the Bible. "A writer
named Q was the actual author," the pastor taught.
He was fond of saying, "You can't say that the Bible is
without error."

Bob and Judy began to express their concerns, calling on their pastor to accept the clear teaching of the
Scriptures as his guide. They wrote:

> We are not being fed from the sermons or asked to
> stretch our faith. We feel that the end times are im-
> minent and wonder about the content of your ser-
> mons. . . . We need to hear about hell and heaven
> and about Satan and about Jesus' victory over sin
> for us!

Today, after reading *Left Behind*, Bob says, "I talk to
Jesus, not about him. I use Scripture, not human
reasoning, to decide an issue. I don't care how people
react to me when I talk about heaven and hell, Jesus as
the only way to God, things like that. My main concern

before was whether or not people liked me. As a new man in Christ, I am much more confrontational with people—especially with the pastor and my fellow elders—concerning the way things get done. After all, choosing elders and deacons is spelled out clearly in Scripture."

Bob and Judy prayed for months about leaving, hoping the church would change. Their love for the people at First Church was strong, but when the pastor told them he would be more comfortable if they were gone, the couple decided it was time.

"That was a heartbreaker," Bob said. "Anymore, we simply tell people we weren't hearing the gospel. Many in Judy's circle of friends at First Church were slipping into New Age practices, which caused her finally to stop attending their monthly women's prayer group.

"We miss the fellowship of everyone, and we pray for them and encourage them when we see them, but Satan is great at blinding people to the truth. Reading *Left Behind* awakened us to our great need."

"Your novels have inspired me to slow down (always a problem for me) and ask, 'What is God calling me to in this situation?' I am trying to stay in conscious contact with God. Every moment provides an opportunity to carry out God's will. Your books have helped me to improve my relationships with others."

—BR. KEVIN F.

"Your books—they're the *greatest* evangelistic tools. Such a door opener to the unsaved where I work!"

—KAREN C.

"I am fifteen years old, and ever since I started reading the Left Behind books, my life is a little easier to work with."

—JAIME B.

THE GREATEST GIFT

WHATEVER IS GOOD AND

PERFECT COMES TO US

FROM GOD ABOVE.

—JAMES 1:17

Little Mary Kay Fry was ready. Scrubbed, pressed, and brushed, she watched down Mead Street for the arrival of Father Mike, who would conduct a special mass in her family's Kalamazoo, Michigan home. The girl's parents beamed as the priest chanted the *Kyrie eleison* ("Lord, have mercy").

Years passed. Mary Kay graduated from Hackett Catholic Central High and entered nurses' training at Nazareth College, a hometown school conveniently affiliated with Borgess Hospital. Marriage, three babies, and duties as a homemaker consumed virtually all of her time, talents, and energy.

She was reading a book entitled *Left Behind* when a friend selling Pampered Chef items for busy home-makers popped in for a visit. The friend noticed Mary Kay's book and inquired about it.

"Oh, that? It's an easy read," Mary Kay said.

"That's all? Just 'an easy read'?" her friend asked.

When Mary Kay shrugged, her friend knew she had some work to do. First, she invited Mary Kay and her husband and sons to attend Richland Bible Church in Kalamazoo. Second, she explained the meaning of the true end-time events fictionalized in *Left Behind*.

Looking back on that momentous conversation, Mary Kay said, "I had a religious upbringing. I believed that Jesus was the Son of God, that he died on the cross to save us from sin. I believed also in the Holy Trinity, but somehow I had completely failed to appropriate that salvation."

She sensed a spiritual stirring when her second son was born, but she did not respond to the Lord's call. Seven years later, when her youngest son was born, she began reading the Left Behind books. The more she read, the more curious she became about what the book of Revelation predicted. She looked up scriptural passages to see whether the issues were invented or authentic.

On January 23, 2000, Mary Kay Farrell was again

sitting in the congregation at Richland Bible Church. When the pastor called for sinners to repent and believe the gospel, she responded. *Left Behind* had sown the seed, her friend had watered it, and now pastor Larry Kiser was reaping the harvest. With a heart full of joy, Mary Kay acknowledged her Lord that day as Savior and prayed the sinner's prayer for salvation.

Today, she juggles household and school responsibilities with three lively sons, plus two Pampered Chef shows each week.

"My father and brother do not believe, but I am hoping that if I can get them to read your books, it will wake them up to the Lord. The waiting list to check out the Left Behind books by marines at Camp Lejeune, North Carolina, is long."

—DEAN S.

"I was introduced to your books by a despised neighbor who yelled unmercifully at his wife. But it was a coworker who gave me seven Left Behind books to read and pass on. Our Lord opened my eyes and heart, giving me a great hunger and opening doors through study of His Word. And I am only *one* person among uncounted others to be touched."

—MARTHA A.

"I had slipped in my faith, but the writings of Messrs. LaHaye and Jenkins helped me back into the frame of mind that I should have been in. I am an inspection supervisor and spend most of my time reading code. But since the Left Behind books came, I've read nearly the entire New Testament and other Christian books. They've opened my eyes to God's love."

—ROBERT P.

GOD AT MIT

TRUTH SOMETIMES NOT

SOUGHT FOR COMES

FORTH TO THE LIGHT.

— MENANDER

During summers between semesters at Anderson University in Indiana, Kristy Boren found work at a computer company in Ellicott City, Maryland. The experience dovetailed nicely with her college major and paid a salary that helped cover her college tuition. There was never any discussion of her Christian faith at work until Michael Artz from MIT arrived.

It didn't take Kristy long to discover that Mike had a philosophy of life quite different from hers. Mike had been raised in the Roman Catholic Church, but he had rebelled against his upbringing during his teen years.

"I've read the Bible," Mike told Kristy. "I've also read the Koran and looked into several other religions."

"So, what are you now?" Kristy inquired.

"I'm a pagan," Mike said proudly. "Paganism, in its many forms, is by far the oldest religion known to man. The more I read about it, the more I'm bothered by Christianity's push to convert and rule people who just want to be left alone. Each Christian holiday is actually just a converted pagan holiday. All the evil done in the name of Christianity—the Crusades, the Spanish Inquisition—well, why believe in something that requires you to force your belief on others?"

He spoke readily of Mother Earth and transcendentalism. Kristy got the impression that Mike had mined the ideas of Aristotle, Archimedes, Aquinas, Apollonius, and Bacon and knew all the poems and plays of Goethe. They didn't talk much about their respective faiths, but whenever they did, Kristy would hear Mike's quiet but adamant opinion that he did not agree with what she believed.

However, Mike and Kristy did agree on one thing—they both liked to read. Often after work they wandered into Borders to spend a couple of hours browsing and, most likely, buying something to take home.

On one of these trips, Kristy came upon the novel

Soul Harvest—fourth in the Left Behind series that focuses on the end times. She had already read the first three books but was unaware that the fourth volume was already in the stores. Excited about the prospect of seeing the world take sides for and against the Antichrist, Kristy tucked the book under her arm and got out her wallet. On the way home she outlined the basic story of the Left Behind books for Mike and suggested he read them. She hoped the books would give Mike a more positive view of Christianity.

The next time they visited the bookstore, Mike bought *Left Behind* and plunged in. Soon afterward, he told Kristy that he had "really enjoyed the book." The plot was "very good" and the Christianity portrayed was "interesting." He also read the second book, *Tribulation Force,* and was ready to read *Nicolae.*

After work one day, Mike was quite eager to buy the third book. Kristy didn't want to make the twenty-five-minute drive to Borders that evening, so she told him about a Christian bookstore five minutes away from his apartment.

"You won't have to announce your religion at the door," she told him with a smile. Mike looked pained but decided to go. Later he admitted, "It wasn't bad."

Several days later, Kristy received an e-mail message from Mike at work. She could tell right away that this message was different from any she'd previously received from him. Instead of joking around, he was quite serious:

I was finishing *Nicolae* last night, and I came across the passage that read, "And now may the Lord bless you and keep you. May the Lord make his face to shine upon you and give you peace." And I started to cry. And I couldn't stop. I don't know why, but I think that I felt something. Felt something greater and more magnificent than I have ever known, than I have ever believed. I have read so much, and come to the conclusion that I was pagan, because that made the most sense to me. Everything fit. It was a totally intellectual decision. Now, I seem to be totally irrational and I can't help it. I *feel,* and that is something that I have never really done in my life before. Having no experience with this, I can only come to one conclusion—that I felt God, that I am a Christian.

Surprise and stunned as she read Mike's e-mail, Kristy went to the washroom and cried for quite a while before responding. She knew that her relationship with Mike had changed forever. Mike later went back to that same Christian bookstore and bought a Bible to take back with him to the campus of MIT, where Mike has maintained his faith in the Savior and thrived.

Kristy sat down that night and wrote to Jerry Jenkins. "Mike's conversion was truly an act of God," she wrote. "I am honored to have played a small part."

Mike Artz began his friendship with Kristy Boren as

"a pagan" and ended up quoting the priestly blessing of Numbers 6:24-26 through tears of conviction. Although human failure and rebellion had darkened his life, God's patience and mercy pierced the gloom to bring comfort to one who turned from his unbelief toward Him.

"These books have made me think long and hard about my relationship with Jesus Christ. As a result, I have rededicated my life to Jesus and been baptized."

—J. C. BURNS

"You've helped me wake up and see how far away from God I was and how much closer I need to be. Everyone who professes to be a Christian needs to read these books."

—JOHN K.

"A few times I caught myself praying for these fictional characters. That's when I knew that you had developed the characters superbly. I, for one, want the series stretched to twenty-four volumes."

—JERRY M.

"Thanks for the wake-up call. I did it! I rededicated my life to Jesus Christ."

—JAMES S.

A LIFE
SURPRISED

AWAKE, ARISE, OR BE

FOREVER FALLEN!

—JOHN MILTON

Christine Ferrin of Holland, Michigan was shopping in a local bookstore one day and bought a copy of *Left Behind.* "I started reading it before I got home," Christine said, "and I didn't want to put it down." She learned that God knows the secrets in our hearts, and He knows who we really are, but He is forgiving. "That just blew me away!" she said. "It was as if I had never heard it before. The stories about Rayford and Buck and Chloe, and all the other characters were intriguing enough, but the verses from the

Bible that Dr. LaHaye and Mr. Jenkins used to support the events were godsends."

When Christine finished reading the book, she didn't want to lay it down. When she turned the final page, she sensed that a new chapter of her life had begun. She had struggled all her life with the mistaken view that she could never be forgiven for her sins. She had lived with the fear that she could never be faithful enough to satisfy a God who is holy and perfect. She knew from experience that even when she tried really hard to be good, eventually her weaknesses would betray her. Surely she would be exposed in the piercing white-hot light of God's judgment. She dreaded Judgment Day because she was sure she would be turned away—the ultimate rejection.

But with her confession of Jesus as her Lord came great joy and freedom from the panic that had gripped her for so long. Now she knew she belonged to Him forever, even after death. No one could separate her from Him. "If the Holy Spirit had a size," Christine said, "He was greater to me that day than the sum of the universe!"

She purchased extra copies of *Left Behind* to distribute among her friends so that they could discover the same joy and be happy, and "finally be able to receive the wonderful message that God has been trying to send them." To know that the One who loved her eternally had been with her all along made Christine feel whole as a person and complete as a believer.

An intense desire to study the Scriptures consumed her. She had never before been so eager to read and study the Bible. God's Word gave her hope and the inspiration to live it out. He refreshed her thirsty soul with living water.

She and her husband, Mark, began to get up early in the morning to enjoy Bible study together and share time over coffee. Verses that once made no sense now became clear. God soon blessed them with a daughter they named Faith Rose, and their joy grew even deeper.

"Just to know that He would take me home to live with all the other believers someday and would not turn me away, well, that strengthens my faith," Christine said. "Isn't that what He promises in Matthew 28:20? 'Teach them to obey everything that I have taught you, and I will be with you always, even until the end of this age'" (NKJV).

Now Christine blesses her fellow believers with the words of the apostle John at the end of Revelation: "The grace of the Lord Jesus be with you all. Amen."

"'Oh, she's Bible-thumping again.' That's what I always said under my breath when Mom read the Left Behind series and started bothering me about salvation. I had never acknowledged the fact of God. In my fifteen-year-old mind, it just didn't seem very important.

"Then I started reading. I never knew how real God is until I started looking up the Scriptures that *Left Behind* referenced. Then I thought, *Hey, maybe it's not just a fairy tale after all!*

"Since then, I've read most of the New Testament, and tonight I'm ready to accept the Lord into my life as my Savior. I have found peace in God."

—DIONNE A.

"I grew up in the deep South and visited a Baptist church occasionally, but never took the final step of accepting Jesus into my life. In a local store, I got this overwhelming feeling that I needed to buy that book in front of me. I took *Left Behind* home, and I have been saved by the blood of the Lamb. Got a whole new outlook on life! The Lord was with you when you wrote that book!"

—T. B.

"If you ever doubt the impact of your books upon the lives of readers, check the amazon.com reviews. You take spiritual truth and change it into interesting, powerful books. These are the best witnessing tools around. If God is for us, who can stand against us?"

—CHRIS S.

"These are the greatest novels I've ever read. I'm a devout Catholic (a convert from a fundamentalist church), so I don't agree exactly on your interpretation of the end times. But these books do a great job in spreading the good news of Jesus Christ, which is more important than whether or not we agree about the end times. Both our churches agree that the most important thing a person can do is to make a commitment to Christ."

—MIKE M.

HOW SWEET
THE SOUND

―――――――――――――――――――――――――――

SAY IT WITH MUSIC.

—IRVING BERLIN

Michael Moore, the grandson of a minister, became an atheist at the age of twenty. "How can there be a God," he demanded of his friends, "when people are needlessly starving to death every day, when children are dying of cancer, and when the Reverend Martin Luther King is gunned down in a senseless act of violence?"

At twenty-three, Michael stood at the altar and promised his bride that he would stay with her "till death do us part." But nineteen years and two children later, no matter how hard he tried, Michael no longer felt he could uphold his vow, so the marriage was over.

On top of that, he was laid off from his job and could not find another. Two years and 266 job applications later, he found himself living in San Francisco, broke, deeply in debt, and disillusioned. "Thank God my children still loved me," he said, "and I had the love and support of friends and family members."

During this awful time, Michael awoke to the spiritual questions we must all face. In the book *A Brief History of Time* by Dr. Stephen Hawking, he saw how preposterous it was to believe that "a cosmic bang, a cloud of dust, and a puff of gas could somehow congeal to become . . . us." On top of this mystery came hints and messages from close friends about truth and morality and the immensity of the universe in a way that Michael had never considered. All this led to his accepting the idea that there were many unexplainable—yes, supernatural—things operating all around us every day.

"Finally," he said, "a friend proved to my satisfaction that Jesus Christ exists, that He created the universe, that He loves me, and that He is willing to forgive my sins."

On March 17, 1996, at a Sunday morning service in Ontario, California, Michael asked Jesus to enter his heart and live within him from then on. Until that moment, he had considered Christian people to be hypocritical, weak, and ineffective. Now he looked at them with the eyes of a brother in Christ.

With joy in his heart, blessed by his new faith, he returned to San Francisco and read everything about

Christianity he could get his hands on. He listened faithfully to KFAX radio, an AM station in Fremont, California that broadcasts Christian programming in the San Francisco Bay Area. After listening during the day to Dr. Charles Stanley, pastor Greg Laurie, Focus on the Family, Hank Hannegraf, and others, Michael would switch to the Internet at night and continue filling his soul with more teaching and testimony.

As Michael pored over the Scriptures, he found that some of the passages in the book of Revelation were fairly difficult to understand. Isaiah and Daniel also had passages that were beyond his grasp.

For Christmas that year, a friend gave him a copy of the novel *Left Behind*.

"I tore through it in two days," Michael said. "I couldn't put it down. Then I had to know the rest of the story, so I raced through *Tribulation Force, Nicolae, Soul Harvest, Apollyon, Assassins, The Indwelling,* and *The Mark.*" Besides being "the most compelling novels I've ever read," he said, the Left Behind series "brought Revelation alive for me." Michael now understands the end times in a clear, organized way.

A job in the Internet music industry finally opened up in Nashville—2,500 miles east—and Michael made the move. Not long after, a friend invited him to a gathering of Christians called New River Fellowship that met in a barn outside of town. Michael found himself immersed in the love and discipleship of a church body with a passion for worshiping and serving

Jesus Christ. On May 7, 2000, having settled into his first "church home," Michael was baptized in the nearby Harpeth River. Michael is wary of survivalists and doomsayers, because he has seen firsthand the negative effect that baseless "sky is falling" talk can have on a family or on society. But he sees the Left Behind series as a pragmatic illustration of how end-time prophecies might play out. "If several Old and New Testament prophets foretell the same end-time picture over the span of several hundred years," Michael said, "that's good enough for me."

"These books have opened my heart, mind, soul, and eyes to the truth of what the Bible teaches. They have pointed me in the right direction."

—KEVIN S.

"I just read in an archived chat on the Left Behind home page that only original Tribulation Force members will make it to the Glorious Appearing. Please, don't kill off Chloe and Buck! That would crush me. I almost cried when Annie died in *The Mark*. I've never been this immersed in a book. You got through to a very stubborn person. God bless you."

—HOLLY G.

A HINDU GETS
THE MESSAGE

NEVER MISTRUST

THE OBVIOUS.

— GALEN

As a flight attendant for United Airlines,
Karma Leigh Allen has given the book *Left Behind* to
passengers all over the world. At home in New York,
Karma gave a copy to her uncle, thinking that perhaps
he might respond to the call of Christ. Her uncle had
married a Hindu woman and embraced Hinduism
because his wife insisted that their children be raised
in her religious heritage.

Karma had observed that the rapture of the church
was an issue that often sparked the first wave of ques-

tions from people to whom she had given one of the books. She wondered how her uncle would deal with that issue.

But her uncle never called and never wrote, because he had misplaced the gift book before he had a chance to read it. Karma made several trips around the world with United Airlines while she waited and prayed. Then, out of the blue, she received a phone call from her Hindu aunt. With urgency in her voice her aunt inquired, "How can I get a copy of *Tribulation Force*?"

Karma shook her head, smiling as she told the story. "I just couldn't believe it. Our faith is so small and we are blind to circumstances when compared to God. Here I am, thinking that the way into that family is through my uncle, and suddenly his wife becomes the seeker—this woman who has been a Hindu all her life. It turns out *she* is the one who is open to receiving the message."

The aunt continued to read the Left Behind series, and so did Karma's two cousins, who were enjoying the kids' series. Now Karma's aunt is talking about Jesus to her husband, her children, and her parents, as well.

"Those books continue to make a major impact on the lives of unbelievers," Karma said. "Some people very quickly come to Christ, while others, being more cautious, take the longer, more labored path. It's great to know, however, that no matter which path we walk, once we are led by the Spirit, the journey always ends in the arms of Jesus."

"I feel like a new man, walking this earth with pride, security, and a new meaning. I feel better about my relationship with my wife. I've got new 'ammunition' for my children as they grow and learn. Thank you."

—TIMOTHY B.

"I mailed a copy of *Left Behind* to my brother, who was practicing 'Vulcanism' (whatever that is). He called me four days later and said he was already into the second book. He thanked me for making him rethink his spiritual choices. It's not 'in your face' religious— it allows you to stand back and think about it rationally once you're open to the idea."

—AARON S.

"My brother, serving a life sentence in a state prison, gave his life to Christ after reading *Left Behind*. I marvel at the transformation within this man."

—DENISE F.

WHEN FRIENDS FORSAKE

WE SHOULD BEHAVE

TO OUR FRIENDS AS WE

WISH OUR FRIENDS TO

BEHAVE TO US.

—ARISTOTLE

Trish Pinolo of Melbourne, Australia, read the final page of *Desecration* and then snapped the book shut. She adjusted her pillow and was leaning over to turn off the light when it suddenly hit her. She opened the book again and reread Tsion's exhortation: "Do not be distracted, beloved, for we rest in the sure promises of the God of Abraham, Isaac, and Jacob that we have been delivered to this place of refuge that cannot be penetrated by the enemy of his Son."

"Why, that's exactly the prayer *I* need to pray," she exclaimed to herself. The struggles she had been facing were—in a certain way of thinking, anyway—not all that different from the challenges facing the tribulation saints who were trying to cope with the Antichrist and his minions. Looking back now, it was fair to say that her life had turned into a kind of tribulation ever since her conversion. After she surrendered her life to the Savior, she was suddenly fired from her job, her brother and sister stopped visiting her altogether, and they never even called to check up on her when she underwent major surgery. They distanced themselves even further when she was diagnosed with clinical depression. With no employment, she had to survive on social security payments received every two weeks. No pastor came calling; no church members brought food and good wishes or promised to pray for her.

"I blamed God," she said, "instead of looking at all this as an opportunity to draw closer to Him."

After her depression was diagnosed, Trish began attending a small church in Melbourne near her apartment, but it brought her even more grief. These folks insisted that she throw out all her prescription drugs, stop seeing doctors, and seek healing through meditation and prayer. There was an ingrained distrust of psychiatrists and antidepressants within this fellowship.

Ironically, one of the pastors in that church took

Trish under his wing to provide counsel and prayer, and his direction made sense of biblical admonitions. Unfortunately, the congregation didn't accept what he said either. When that pastor left the church, so did Trish. She had had enough of their put-downs and judgments.

Although she withdrew from fellowship, Trish continued to play Christian music in spite of her distrust and anger. And just in case God might be listening, she also breathed a prayer now and then.

When *Desecration*, the ninth novel of the Left Behind series, arrived, it was "perfectly timed," she said, "to restore my faith in God. Instead of listening to people who are prone to making the same mistakes I do, I began taking everything to Christ and asking Him for guidance and help. It's as if I had discovered anew the faith and love for Christ I'd found earlier. I again have fallen in love with God. I have learned to trust Him completely and not to listen to Satan's lies."

In a recent e-mail message, she wrote:

> I will no longer be so foolish as to walk away from Christ. That was the worst time of my life. I have learned that no problem or sin is so great that the Father cannot forgive, if I just hand it over to Him. After all, I cannot hide anything from Him. He is the Alpha and the Omega so He knows all of my upcoming struggles and sins before I do. If I confess it and give it over, it makes my life a lot easier

to handle. I don't have to struggle alone. Thank
God I found the Left Behind books to put this all
into perspective and give me hope.

"I had tried numerous times to open up the book of Revelation but always got so lost and confused that I shut the book in frustration. Now, when I am having a good day with my temporal lobe epilepsy, I can open it and, because of you, I can grasp a lot more of what it is actually saying. So, in this life of frustration that I now live in (not knowing what my malady will do to me from one day to the next because of seizures), I want to say thank you for your help in keeping me hungry for the Word and for brightening some of my darker days."

—MARSHA M.

"How grateful I am for your novels. I have, after all these years, just begun to read *Left Behind*. I knew in my heart I was supposed to read it from the beginning. I have been away from God for a number of years. Your novels have been instrumental in helping me go back to the Father who, I know, loves me."

—SALLY L.

"I'm a high school senior, raised a Catholic. I stopped attending church soon after my father died of leukemia when I was six. My mom tried, but eventually realized that I would simply cry through masses and sulk for days afterward. Your novels have renewed for me the faith that I lost long ago. I went back to mass with my mother for the first time in about eight years. Your book, and the support of friends who attend church, made me take that step."

—JENNIFER C.

PART FIVE

KIDS IN THE KINGDOM

Young men and maidens . . .

Let them all praise the name of the Lord.

Psalm 148:12–13

THE BOY WHO LOVED SATAN

SATAN FINDS SOME

MISCHIEF STILL FOR IDLE

HANDS TO DO.

—ISAAC WATTS

In 1990, when he was twelve years old, Corey Walmsley's world crumbled. His beloved grandpa died, his parents filed for divorce, and personal disappointments shook his Christian faith apart.

Always the type to look at things objectively, the young man from Horton, Michigan, decided—tragically—that God must hate him. He would therefore give his allegiance to Satan and willingly "hate

God back." His mind was made up, but he decided to hide his decision from his friends.

Corey began reading books written by the founder of the Satanic Church. Eventually, Corey announced to his friends his newfound allegiance to Lucifer. In high school, he read books on satanic witchcraft, rituals, and myths. If anyone frowned at him in class, Corey would keep reading and tell them to bug off.

In the hallway one day, a disapproving classmate growled, "Satanic punk!" Corey grabbed him by the throat and slammed him against a locker. "You've got thirty seconds to apologize," he hissed, "or I'll kill you."

A teacher passing by rushed to stop Corey, but he quickly shoved her out of the way. Nevertheless, the interruption was long enough to cause him to take stock of what he was doing.

"I saw what I was becoming," he said. "I felt as if I was losing my humanity."

Not long after that, a friend named Jim asked Corey to go to church with him.

"I had to respect anyone that brave," Corey said. "I just laughed and walked away."

But Jim grabbed his shoulder and spun him around. "Okay, but make me a promise."

"Like what?"

"If you ever do go to church, you'll go to mine."

Corey laughed again. "Pretty funny." But then he thought a moment and shrugged. "It's a deal." They shook hands and went their separate ways, but Corey was still laughing inside. He knew he would *never* be caught dead in a church.

As he got older, his mother began to be afraid of him. High school classmates were careful not to get too close to him. They had seen his angry outbursts.

Months later, after he had forgotten about his promise to Jim, a friend named Mike made a bet with him. If Corey lost, he would attend church with him. The bet was that Corey couldn't manipulate a friend of theirs with his "satanic influence" into going out with a certain classmate. The wager sounded ridiculous, so Corey grabbed his friend's hand and shook it. But Corey lost the bet, and the following Sunday he found himself sitting with his friend in his church, feeling foolish. Afterward Mike asked, "How'd you like it?"

"I dunno," Corey said. "I slept through the whole service."

When Jim heard about it, he confronted Corey. "Wait a minute, remember our deal?" he asked. "You said if you ever *did* go to church, you'd go to *mine*."

"All right," Corey grumbled. The next Sunday he kept his promise and went with Jim to church. Inside, Corey was boiling, feeling tricked. He decided going in that he would have some fun by disrupting the service.

"So, I'm sitting there listening to the pastor and suddenly I become speechless," Corey said, remembering that Sunday morning. "Everything he said seemed to be directed right at me. Intrigued, I returned the following Sunday." He told himself that he just wanted more stuff to laugh at.

After four Sundays, Jim gave Corey a copy of *Left Behind* and told him to read it.

"The book scared me big time," Corey said. "I had to face the truth. I decided to become a Christian and get baptized right away. The part that got my attention was the chaos during the Rapture and the accidents and deaths. I decided that I would rather not be there to go through all that.

"*Left Behind* had the greatest impact on me because it showed me that Jesus could come at any time," Corey said. "And after the Rapture, the world will be in complete chaos. I gave myself over to the Lord." Corey threw out all his CDs, magazines, and books with satanic themes—"anything that would hold me to the old life. For the first time," he said, "I felt love for people other than myself. My mother and sister saw the change in my life as time went on. Today they are happy and attend church with me. Jesus gave me not only salvation but also the one thing that I've wanted my whole life—happiness. For that I am eternally grateful.

"Since I've been saved, people have told me that my testimony about how Christ changed my life is inspirational. As a Satanist, I always tried to turn people away from God. That will always be a burden on my heart and soul. I hope to show as many people as possible that Jesus is the only hope for them. And when the Lord comes, I hope He will be proud of me. I know God has forgiven me, but I can only forgive myself with His help. The only way I can redeem my past is to try to win as many people to Christ as possible."

"I've been reading Left Behind: The Kids to my third graders, a chapter each day after lunch. One day as I finished, a student came to my desk and asked, 'Can we pray now in case someone in our class has never asked Jesus into their hearts and are afraid they will get left behind?'

"'Of course!' I said. So two of the children knelt at their desks, then a few more, until all of my students were kneeling. I knelt, too, as I began the sinner's prayer, asking the Lord to give each child assurance that he or she would be safe and would not be left behind when our Savior comes for His own.

"When we finished, we all stood up. One child said, 'Can we raise our hand if we just asked Jesus into our heart?'

"Again I said, 'Of course!' Three students raised their hands. Then I looked out over my class and said, 'If you are going to be with Jesus when he comes back, raise your hand.' Everyone did! I was so excited that just the retelling of the story gives me goose bumps. Our God is so good."

In His love,

JANE M.

"My brother is also reading the books, but I stayed up all night and left him to catch up. Nobody else in our family is a Christian. Hopefully after they read this book, they will be. It's late here in the UK, so I'm going to bed."

—JEREMY F.

"I got fourteen of the books in the children's series, one for every year I have lived. Last night when I finished the twelfth book, I broke down and cried at the end, but I felt so good that I had grown closer to God while reading them. I used to complain about having to go to church; now I beg every Sunday to go and learn about the Lord. I know your books are fiction, but now I feel like I know what's coming and I'm ready."

—JESSICA

SCARED
STRAIGHT

NO ACT OF KINDNESS IS

EVER WASTED.

—AESOP

When Amanda was still in elementary school, she often woke up at night and cried because she knew that someday she was going to die.

"I didn't understand death and I didn't know about God," she said. "Sometimes when my family would talk about the end of the world, my dad would say that a whole bunch of things were supposed to take place before the end came. I always asked what, but he never answered me in depth." One day her father taught her a prayer, but "he neglected to introduce me to the One I was praying to," she said. Here is that brief prayer:

> Angel of God, my guardian dear,
> To God's love commit me here.

As a freshman in high school, Amanda heard her mother reading *Left Behind* in the kitchen one night to her older sister. She was blown away. People disappearing? The Bible foretelling it? A Tribulation? An Antichrist? The message of the book frightened her mother so badly that she stopped reading it and laid it aside. But Amanda took it to her room and gobbled it up in four days.

When she shared the message of the book with a friend at school, her classmate began avoiding her and writing nasty e-mail messages "seething with profanity." She said the message of *Left Behind* made her feel "dirty." When Amanda pointed out that everything was in the Bible, her friend accused her of "closed-circuit thinking."

Her brother took a look at *Left Behind* but tossed it aside as "just some pathetic God book."

Amanda read all the books that were available in the series up to that point in just three months, and felt that God had brought them to her attention in a special act of kindness. "There was no other way to explain it," she said. And yet, she hesitated to give her heart to Christ. A Christian girl in her French class told her she "couldn't wait to disappear."

"Well, *I'm* not going," Amanda said. The girl invited Amanda to her church, but her mother wouldn't let her go.

Then one day Amanda found a brochure on the floor of a Kmart store. It featured a comic strip telling about a girl who had cancer and almost died without knowing Jesus. Standing there in that store, Amanda took stock of her life: *If I die without Christ, or if the Rapture came right when I was on the brink of decision, I would miss it,* she thought. She became a Christian that very day.

Her family was not as ready to make the decision. "They needed help," she said. "My brother rationalized away the teachings of the Bible. He even grabbed my Bible away from me one night when I was reading and threw it on the floor. My whole family has seen the movie *Left Behind,* yet they criticize me for reading the book. Some friends almost abandoned me when I tried to bring them to Christ."

Amanda told another good friend at school about God, but her friend laughed at her. "I think it would be amusing to go through the Tribulation," she said. Amanda bought her a copy of the book, but her friend wouldn't read it. "Why won't you read it?" Amanda asked.

"Because," she said, "it's scary. I'm just not a God person."

"Well, maybe you better become one," Amanda warned. "The world *is* becoming scary. Isn't that all the more reason to reach out to God?" But they never talked about that again.

Amanda started reading her Bible to her friend, but "she just kinda drifted." Sometimes, Amanda said, "I just feel like Rayford when Chloe refused to commit. I mean, you *care* about these people so much, and when they refuse to see the truth, it really hurts."

She made a bunch of flyers about God's love and hung them around school, but they were quickly taken down. She surrounded herself with students who were brothers and sisters in Christ. Together they tried to get a Christian club started on campus to spread the word, but "it hasn't gotten off the ground yet."

Next year when she turns sixteen and gets her driver's license, Amanda wants to attend New Covenant Bible Church. "I really want to be a Christian author," she said, "so I can help people the way Tim LaHaye and Jerry B. Jenkins helped me. I've won a few writing contests, so I guess that means I'm all right as a writer. I started writing a book. I also want to become a psychologist."

"I'm only fourteen, and there are probably younger people than me reading these books. It is also encouraging to me because I'm a writer also. I'm going to put a lot more effort behind my work because I have seen what it can accomplish. Do you also write poetry?"

—KRISTEN T.

"I'm thirteen and in Tennessee. I used to hate reading, but after I started reading my dad's copy of *Left Behind,* I just wanted to keep reading to see what happens to Buck and Chloe. I realized that no matter how many times I fall, I must get back up. My brother David is the only one in my family not reading your books."

—KEITH S.

"The Left Behind books have helped me with my religion and with my reading skills. I am an eighth grader at St. Mary's in North Little Rock. Since I have started reading these books, I have achieved higher grades in school and have become more interested in religion and Christ. I love to hear about Revelation and the end of the world. It has changed a lot of troubles in my life into better things."

—PAIGE S.

MY LIFE SWERVED OUT OF CONTROL

I HAVE HIDDEN YOUR

WORD IN MY HEART. . .

—PSALM 119:11

"When I was in fourth grade," said Daniel Aartman, "a lot of my classmates were reading Left Behind: The Kids. I was curious, so I checked one out at the library." Daniel became so interested in the series that he finished sixteen books in five months. Then he started reading the adult books and soon completed *Left Behind, Tribulation Force, Nicolae, Soul Harvest,* and *Apollyon.*

"I was saved when I was three," he said. "When I was older, I won a mountain bike for memorizing verses from the Bible, and I even won the "Spirit Award" in third grade, but I never had a personal relationship with Jesus Christ. My life swerved out of control so much that I was overcome and just burst out in tears one night in bed. After that, I realized that Jesus could help with all my problems."

Daniel now tries to be a witness in everything he does. He is currently trying to share the gospel with a friend on his swim team. "It is a real challenge," he says.

"A lot of my friends like to read the Left Behind: The Kids books. We like to compare our opinions about them. I plan to read all of the Left Behind books. They are getting very interesting."

"I'm fourteen, and I've always gone to church. But I never understood what was happening, and I never knew God. When reading #12 of the kids series, I decided to pray. Do you have any time to e-mail me . . . ?"

—KATIE K.

"These books have opened my heart, mind, soul, and eyes to the truth of what the Bible teaches. They have pointed me in the right direction."

—KEVIN S.

"Your books changed my life. Left Behind: The Kids is awesome. I read all four books in two days. I need *more!* Now I'm not afraid of His return.

—JESSI M., AGE 12

"Hi. I'm thirteen. I read the adult *Left Behind* before the kids' books. I went to church and thought I knew it all, but it never really got to me. I don't think I would have been saved if not for you. I bought a Bible. Thank you. You saved my life."

—BILLY P.

HOT TUB TOPICS

DON'T LET ANYONE THINK

LESS OF YOU BECAUSE

YOU ARE YOUNG.

BE AN EXAMPLE

TO ALL BELIEVERS . . .

IN THE WAY YOU LIVE.

—1 TIMOTHY 4:12

Daniel, a preacher's kid in San Diego, was in a holding pattern. There was no rebellion, no drinking, no drugs, no bad relationships with girls, but his parents feared that he was "running in neutral, holding something back."

His father took him to a restaurant for breakfast every Saturday morning for man-to-man talks. They visited way past dark in the backyard hot tub until their fingers wrinkled and their faces turned red. They read he-man books about Christian discipleship and tinkered with tools together at the garage workbench. Still, Danny remained conspicuously uncommitted.

Then he found *Left Behind*. For two nights he stayed up late to get through the book. By the time he finished, everything had changed. Soon, Saturday morning breakfast conversations focused on *Tribulation Force, Nicolae,* and *Soul Harvest*. Hot tub topics suddenly turned to the Rapture, the Antichrist, and the Tribulation. Danny had finally gotten out of neutral and was quickly gaining speed. His father had to run to keep up.

One Sunday evening, Danny brought two unsaved buddies to church. At the invitation, he pointed them to the altar to come to Christ, and both boys did.

"I personally want to offer the publisher a million thank-yous from me and my wife," the pastor wrote. "You have helped make our prayers come true! It's as if Danny were right there in the Tribulation Force, marching through the Chicago airport arm-in-arm with Rayford, Chloe, Buck, and Bruce, ready to fight the enemies of God in whatever challenge lies ahead."

"My sister and brother-in-law are now saved because they read the books. Thanks be to God above for allowing me the privilege of seeing some of my family members come to Christ. My mother is reading them. I'm hopeful!"

—JESSICA J.

"Even though I am eleven years old, I can relate to Judd because I want to preach to everybody in school. I have to be careful not to draw people away from Christ. Judd feels the same way. I imagine myself as each kid."

—BRANDON S.

"I realize that what happened to the kids could happen to me. I'm thirteen, a fresh, new believer, and it's all due to your books. If you want to, write me back."

—ELIZABETH M.

LIVING FOR
JESUS

─────────────────

THE LORD IS FAITHFUL; HE

WILL MAKE YOU STRONG

AND GUARD YOU FROM

THE EVIL ONE.

—2 THESSALONIANS 3:3

When Matthew Dutton's fourth-grade teacher
in Dallas, Texas, invited her class to bring their favorite
book to class for her to read, she received a small
library of possibilities from enthusiastic youngsters.
Matthew brought one of the episodes from the Left
Behind: The Kids series, telling the teacher it was "a
great book."

The teacher, who is a Christian, took her pupil aside. "Matthew," she said, her voice low, "I cannot read this book."

"Why?" Matthew asked.

"Well, we are forbidden by this school to read any Christian books," she said. "Furthermore, we can't pray to Jesus or even talk about Him in class."

At home that evening, Matthew reported his teacher's decision. "Yeah," said his little brother, Aaron. "And the kids make fun of me when I pray at lunch."

After dinner their mother, Julia, sat on the edge of the lower bunk in her sons' room and read the next installment of the Left Behind: the Kids series for her kids.

Night after night, Julia read each of the books in succession. The books were a much-needed encouragement for Julia as well as her sons. Julia had been diagnosed with fibromyalgia and also suffered from chronic inflammation in her spine. And her troubles didn't end there. One night after she had finished reading book nineteen in the series, Julia had to explain to her sons that their father would no longer be living at home with them. It had all happened so quickly, and she hadn't wanted to surprise them right after school.

"Facing our divorce was an experience only God could have taken my children through," Julia said. "When they came home and saw some furniture missing and other items rearranged, they were more concerned about me than about the house. The books have definitely made us all stronger Christians," Julia said. "I see how important it is to live for Jesus. These heroes in the Left Behind: The Kids series offer examples to my sons, showing how it is done. I only pray that they see a difference in my life, too."

"You have hooked another reader. This series has given me a boot to be more evangelistic in my prayers, thoughts, and conversations."

—ROBERT B.

"A mother called her nine-year-old boy at his grandma's house to see if he had avoided a couple of little boys who always helped him get into trouble. He said he had, except maybe for lunchtime when he discovered they didn't know they could get left behind in the Rapture. He had run home to read his Bible to get more stuff to tell his friends tomorrow."

—BILLIE G.

"I'm fourteen, and I love Left Behind: The Kids. I've read them all. Also the Left Behind graphic novels. I am a new Christian. These books helped me to realize that I needed Jesus. Will I be left behind? Well, now that I am a Christian I know that if Jesus comes back in my lifetime, I will be gone! Keep up the good work."

—HEATHER A.

"I am not a teen, I'm thirty-seven, yet I have enjoyed the kids' books. It's a great way to help people learn more about the Bible and things to come."

—JANIS D.

"Through these books I have found faith in Jesus Christ. I try to live every day to my best because I know He is watching. Thanks! Funny, I grew up in Waukegan and now reside in Wadsworth. A lot of the story takes place nearby."

—JIM C.

ABOUT THE AUTHORS

Jerry B. Jenkins (www.jerryjenkins.com) is the writer of the Left Behind series. He owns the Jerry B. Jenkins Christian Writers Guild, an organization dedicated to mentoring aspiring authors. Former vice president for publishing for the Moody Bible Institute of Chicago, he also served many years as editor of *Moody* magazine and is now Moody's writer-at-large.

His writing has appeared in publications as varied as *Reader's Digest, Parade, Guideposts,* in-flight magazines, and dozens of other periodicals. Jenkins's biographies include books with Billy Graham, Hank Aaron, Bill Gaither, Luis Palau, Walter Payton, Orel Hershiser, and Nolan Ryan, among many others. His books appear regularly on the *New York Times, USA Today, Wall Street Journal,* and *Publishers Weekly* best-seller lists.

Jerry is also the writer of the nationally syndicated sports story comic strip *Gil Thorp,* distributed to newspapers across the United States by Tribune Media Services.

Jerry and his wife, Dianna, live in Colorado and have three grown sons.

Dr. Tim LaHaye (www.timlahaye.com), who conceived the idea of fictionalizing an account of the Rapture and the Tribulation, is a noted author, minister, and nationally recognized speaker on Bible prophecy. He is the founder of both Tim LaHaye Ministries and The Pre-Trib Research Center.

He also recently cofounded the Tim LaHaye School of Prophecy at Liberty University. Presently Dr. LaHaye speaks at many of the major Bible prophecy conferences in the U.S. and Canada, where his current prophecy books are very popular.

Dr. LaHaye holds a doctor of ministry degree from Western Theological Seminary and a doctor of literature degree from Liberty University. For twenty-five years he pastored one of the nation's outstanding churches in San Diego, which grew to three locations. It was during that time that he founded two accredited Christian high schools, a Christian school system of ten schools, and Christian Heritage College.

Dr. LaHaye has written over forty books that have been published in more than thirty languages. He has written books on a wide variety of subjects, such as family life, temperaments, and Bible prophecy. His current fiction works, the Left Behind series, written with Jerry B. Jenkins, continue to appear on the best-seller lists of the Christian Booksellers Association, *Publishers Weekly, Wall Street Journal, USA Today,* and the *New York Times.*

He is the father of four grown children and grandfather of nine. Snow skiing, waterskiing, motorcycling, golfing, vacationing with family, and jogging are among his leisure activities.

IN ONE CATACLYSMIC MOMENT
MILLIONS AROUND THE WORLD DISAPPEAR

Experience the suspense of the end times for yourself. The best-selling Left Behind series is now available in hardcover, softcover, and large-print editions.

1
LEFT BEHIND®
A novel of
the earth's last
days . . .

2
**TRIBULATION
FORCE**
The continuing
drama of those
left behind . . .

3
NICOLAE
The rise of
Antichrist . . .

4
**SOUL
HARVEST**
The world
takes sides . . .

5
APOLLYON
The Destroyer is
unleashed . . .

6
ASSASSINS
Assignment:
Jerusalem,
Target: Antichrist

7
**THE
INDWELLING**
The Beast takes
possession . . .

8
THE MARK
The Beast rules
the world . . .

9
DESECRATION
Antichrist takes
the throne . . .

10
**THE
REMNANT**
On the brink of
Armageddon . . .

11
ARMAGEDDON
The cosmic battle
of the ages . . .

ABRIDGED AUDIO Available on three CDs or two cassettes for each title. (Books 1–9 read by Frank Muller, one of the most talented readers of audio books today.)

AN EXPERIENCE IN SOUND AND DRAMA Dramatic broadcast performances of the best-selling Left Behind series. Twelve half-hour episodes on four CDs or three cassettes for each title.

GRAPHIC NOVELS Created by a leader in the graphic novel market, the series is now available in this exciting new format.

LEFT BEHIND®: THE KIDS Four teens are left behind after the Rapture and band together to fight Satan's forces in this series for ten- to fourteen-year-olds.

LEFT BEHIND® > THE KIDS < LIVE-ACTION AUDIO Feel the reality, listen as the drama unfolds. . . . Twelve action-packed episodes available on four CDs or three cassettes.

CALENDARS, DEVOTIONALS, GIFT BOOKS . . .

FOR THE LATEST INFORMATION ON INDIVIDUAL PRODUCTS, RELEASE DATES, AND FUTURE PROJECTS, VISIT

www.leftbehind.com

Sign up and receive free e-mail updates!